GREAT LIVES IN BRIEF
A New Series of Biographies

ACCURACY

BREVITY · CLARITY

MULTUM
IN PARVO

These are BORZOI BOOKS
Published by ALFRED A. KNOPF *in New York*

JULIUS CÆSAR

Julius Cæsar

A GREAT LIFE IN BRIEF

BY

Alfred Duggan

New York   ALFRED A. KNOPF   1955

L. C. catalog card number: 54–7217

© Alfred Duggan, 1955

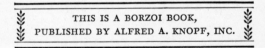

THIS IS A BORZOI BOOK,
PUBLISHED BY ALFRED A. KNOPF, INC.

FIRST EDITION

NOTE ON PROPER NAMES

I have made a point of using the Latin version of all Roman names. We often talk of Pompey and Mark Antony, but then comes the question of where to draw the line; Livius is Livy, but is Cicero Tully? It seemed better, in a book which will be full of Latin names anyway, to stick to the spelling used by contemporary Romans. I have not been so careful with Greek or barbarian names, because in our Roman alphabet we cannot get them completely right even if we try.

Geographical names are always a bother, and it is very hard to be consistent. In general I have used the modern names for well-known places in Europe; but where a famous Roman or Greek name has no famous modern equivalent I have kept the old. There is probably an Arab village on the site of Thapsus, but the name on a printed page would not recall Cæsar's famous battle even to the highly educated.

Asia is used in the Roman sense, meaning what we now call Asia Minor.

Africa is also used in the Roman sense, to mean Tunisia in particular, and loosely all the south coast of the Mediterranean between Egypt and Tangier.

CONTENTS

CONTENTS

JULIUS CÆSAR

CHAPTER ONE

THE SETTING

CIVILIZATION arose about 5,000 years before Christ, when over a wide arc of land between the Caucasus and the Red Sea men began to till the soil; and because they tilled the soil their permanent villages slowly increased to cities. To a primitive mind agriculture is obviously a divine activity. The god makes the seedcorn grow in the ground; he also controls the seasons, and you must plant and weed, or in a more advanced culture plow the field, at the time arranged by the divine calendar. So these early cities were ruled by their gods, through human intermediaries. Sometimes the human intermediary was himself a god, like the Pharaoh of Egypt; sometimes, as in the Sumerian cities, he was the high priest, who alone could communicate with heaven. But in either case the source of his power was supernatural; it had nothing to do with his prowess in war. Probably the last remaining representative of these divine rulers is the Emperor of Japan.

But our Mediterranean civilization early branched off from this stem, which continued unchanged in the Far East. Barbarians from the north made war on the divine cities, and the Near East in the second millennium before Christ was as ravaged by merciless armies as Europe in recent times. The unfortified palaces of Crete perished in fire and bloody sack, but on the coasts of the Ægean the cities were strongly walled. Their walls were breached when the invaders broke in; but the towering stone fortifications remained, as in Argos and Mycenæ they still remain. They were too valuable to be wasted; when refugees had gathered within them, and had learned by a few simple rules to live in peace together behind the wall, the city-state was born.

By 800 B.C. the eastern Mediterranean was ringed with city-states, the direct ancestors of our present civiliza- tion. The marks of a city-state are these: It is a joint company of unlimited liability, whose inhabitants face at least slavery, if not death, if their city should be de- feated in war. It has been founded on a definite date by a definite man, hero, or demigod (unlike the divine cities, which were believed to have existed since the creation of the world). Its first inhabitants had come into the shelter of the walls by a definite and voluntary act of will, and usually they had come from somewhere else (the Athenians claimed to have lived in Attica as long as their cousins the grasshoppers, but even they had deserted certain scattered villages to gather under the rock of the Acropolis). The city is under the special protection of a god, or of a group of gods, who are bound to foster its prosperity so long as the citizens pay them due honor. Of course all these rights and obliga- tions descend to the children of the original settlers. As a rule there is some machinery for admitting adult re- cruits; but it is a complicated machinery, seldom used. Citizenship is a valuable gift, not to be lightly bestowed.

In July 100 B.C. Caius Julius Cæsar was born a citizen of Rome, which was still regarded as a city-state, though its magistrates ruled from Gibraltar to the Black Sea. The Romans knew a great deal about their past history, and this knowledge affected their actions in everyday political life. They may have been mistaken in some of their facts, but that is not important; what matters is the history Cæsar was taught, for unless we also know it we cannot understand his career.

What follows is an outline of what young Caius would have learned at his mother's knee, before he began his formal education. Every Roman citizen knew the same story.

There was once a man named Romulus, whose mother was descended from the kings of the ancient Latin city of Alba Longa, and so from Æneas, who fled from Troy; but his father was Mars, the wargod. Divine omens commanded him to found a city, and on the 21st of April 753 B.C. he plowed round the Palatine Hill in Rome a sacred furrow, called the Pomœrium, to mark the line of his wall. The Pomœrium was the real boundary of the city, though by the time Caius was born it had been enlarged to take in all the Seven Hills of which the Palatine was one. Within it no citizen might carry arms, and a citizen who happened to be an officer might not give orders to a citizen who happened to be serving in the ranks; no blood might be shed, and if an execution should be regrettably necessary it must be carried out beyond the boundary. For the whole city was one household, with its household gods in the temples on the Capitol; Jupiter and Juno, the skygod

and his wife; Mars, the wargod; and Janus, the god of
gates and boundaries. The city had its common hearth,
where a perpetual fire was tended by the priestesses of
Vesta, in origin the young unmarried daughters of the
King. The city had its common hall, the Forum, where
everybody met to hear the instructions of the head of the
family, the King, and to plan the work of the day.

When Romulus founded this city, this large-scale
household fortified by a wall, he peopled it first with his
own followers, the Men of the Wide Plain, or Latins,
who came from the level Campagna south of the Tiber.
But they were too few to found an independent state,
and they had near neighbors whom it was important to
conciliate; so they joined forces with a group of Sabines
from the eastern hills. But even then the new city was
not big enough to stand by itself; so Romulus opened it
to fugitives from anywhere, if they were strong men fit
to bear arms.

Thus Rome was founded, amid a blaze of favorable
omens which showed that she was destined to rule the
world. There was no other reason to suppose so. The
Capitol was a strong citadel, the plain to the south and
east was good for growing corn. But good cornlands and
a strong fortress were the minimum essentials for a city;
every town in Italy shared these advantages.

In fact Rome started under certain handicaps, one
being that in summer the climate is too hot for health.
But worse than the unhealthy atmosphere was the exposed strategic situation. Rome lay on the northern border
of Latium, the Wide Plain. To the south were their

friendly though jealous Latin cousins, and to the west was the sea; but filling all the eastern horizon were the forest-clad hills of the wild Sabines and Samnites, uncouth cattle-raiders who did not live in cities; and just across the fords of the Tiber lay the realm of the gloomy and uncanny Etruscans.

The early Roman state was governed by the constitution common to all new cities. Romulus the founder was of course king, which gave him command in war and responsibility for day-to-day administration. But as he had no paid soldiers, he could not govern against the will of any substantial proportion of his subjects. He heeded the advice of a council of elders, exactly as did the kings in Homer's *Iliad*; this council was called the Senate, and it seems to have been composed of heads of great families who sat by right, and of certain others chosen by the king. But the principle business of Rome from the earliest times was war, and the chief duty of the citizen was to fight in his proper place in the ranks.

A wise ruler knows that it is dangerous to go to war unless the army is willing to fight. So when the whole body of Roman citizens assembled armed in their ranks, as they did frequently for training even in peacetime, the king would ask their opinion on questions of foreign policy. From that it was a short step to seeking their assent to important changes in the law.

The Roman constitution, under the monarchy, was thus of the mixed type which Aristotle thought the best. The king ruled, with the advice of his Senate of elders; but also with the consent of the armed citizens assembled in their ranks; and if it ever came to serious disagreement, the ultimate physical force would rest with the armed citizens.

The popular assembly, which was called the *Comitia*, was divided into voting units called centuries, each supposed to be "worth" a hundred horsemen or knights. A century of knights was a hundred strong, but a century of heavy infantry was more numerous, and a century of light-armed skirmishers many more again. Each century had one vote, no matter how many citizens it contained; thus property was given its due voice in affairs.

The conception of representative government was unknown to the ancient world. No Roman would trust another to represent him and it was understood, at least when issues of general importance were at stake, that unless the citizen came to the Comitia in person he could not vote.

Rome flourished under seven kings. In the year 510 B.C. the last king, Tarquinius Superbus, was driven out because he interfered with the private lives of his subjects. That was the one thing that Romans would not stand; they would obey laws, and in fact they excelled at the kind of public-spirited behavior and consideration for the rights of fellow citizens which made a crowded community run smoothly; but every Roman hated to be told, by a particular individual who was just another human being, to stop what he was doing and do something else immediately.

When the kings had been driven out, the Romans

had to devise a constitution. Like the English, they disliked the idea of scrapping an ancient form if extensive alterations could make it useful. So they kept as much of the old constitution as possible: the Comitia; the ranking of citizens according to property, which made the knights a privileged class; the Senate, which met every day to advise on the running of affairs. But at the top, where the king had been, there was a gap.

The royal power was not diminished; instead it was multiplied. One of the king's functions was to sacrifice to the gods on behalf of the whole people; this power was now entrusted to a king for religious affairs only, the *Rex Sacrorum*, who held office for life but had no power to do anything except sacrifice.

Another very important office of the king was the assignment of citizens to their ranks in the army and so to their voting-centuries; and the nomination of those Senators who were not heads of clans. To perform this function the Roman people elected a *Censor*. His position was, according to the strict theory of the constitution, one of the most dignified in the state, for it was closely bound up with religion. His duties were to count the citizens and then assign them to their centuries; also, he could censure the conduct of any citizen, appoint eminent citizens who were not the heads of clans to the Senate, and remove from the Senate any Senator who behaved disgracefully.

We have left until the last the most vital power of the monarchy, the command of the army, the actual right to say to a particular citizen that he must stand as sentry on one spot until relieved, or get up early for parade when he would rather lie in bed. This power to give orders to individuals was known as the *Imperium*, the right to command. No constitution has ever succeeded in harmonizing the necessary absolute command in war with the theoretical liberty of the citizen; it is a problem that cannot be solved logically, and the Romans got round it by granting the Imperium, the power to command, to several people at once, for a short period.

Every year the Comitia elected two *Consuls*. Each had absolute power, including the power of life and death over soldiers in the field; but either could countermand the orders of the other, and it was the duty of the citizen to obey the last order he received. It was felt that if a Consul was tempted to make himself an unconstitutional ruler he would be thwarted by his equal colleague; also a year was not long enough for him to gather a party of devoted adherents, and he would fear prosecution when his term was up.

Less then the Consuls were the *Prætors*, eight in number, who sat as judges in Rome or took charge of the less important provinces. They also held the Imperium, the power to give orders; but only in the absence of a Consul, whose orders they must obey if he were present.

All these officials were endowed with the full kingly power, which was not divided. The Romans knew that it would be very awkward if officials of equal power constantly countermanded the orders of their colleagues. But that also made it difficult for one elected official to seize permanent power for himself, and they were prepared to put up with a good deal of inefficiency for the sake of continued liberty.

If affairs went very badly and it seemed that the city might be conquered, the Consuls could advise the appointment of a *Dictator*. A Dictator was elected by the Comitia for a term of six months; the whole Imperium was concentrated in his hands. In early Roman history Dictators were rare, and when Cæsar was born the few of them mentioned in the records had always resigned their powers peacefully after six months.

Lesser officials included the *Ædiles*, who looked after temples and houses, and at the bottom of the pyramid of authority the *Quæstors*, whose duty was to keep accounts for the senior magistrates.

One obvious danger in this constitution was that a popular leader might get himself elected again and again, so that in practice he never went out of office. That would happen in a modern state, where parties are organized. But it was thought that serving Consuls would be too busy to canvass, and that without canvassing they would stand no chance of re-election.

CHAPTER TWO

THE RISE OF PARTY

IN 500 B.C. this little republic started its career with an unworkable constitution, an exposed strategic situation, and no military or financial advantages over its neighbors. By 100 B.C. it was the strongest power in the Mediterranean world. There is no material explanation for this success. We can only say that Rome grew great because her soldiers fought very bravely and her politicians never pushed their differences to extremes. Civil wars came later in plenty, but only after the City was supreme; and I hope to be able to show that these wars were not fought for base economic reasons.

There were plenty of causes for political dispute. At the very beginning, while Rome was asserting her mastery over the other cities of the Latin League (cities which lay less than a day's march from her gates), there arose a bitter contest between the Patricians and the Plebeians. This is often regarded as an ordinary quarrel between rich and poor; it was in fact something more complicated. The Patricians, who were decreasing in number, had their own rites of burial and marriage, and they believed that only Patricians could perform the sacrifices on which depended the welfare of the State. Yet if only Patricians could perform the sacrifices, then only Patricians could be magistrates; it followed that at the annual elections every citizen might vote, but he must vote for a Patrician candidate.

Rome seemed headed for civil war. But the dispute was ended, with complete victory for the Plebeians, by the typical Roman method of a peaceful strike. The Plebeians marched off in a body to a neighboring hill, where they threatened to found a new city of their own. That would have destroyed Rome, and the Patricians were deeply patriotic; an embassy begged the strikers to return.

The result was an important change in the constitution. Plebeians were permitted to perform the state sacrifices, and henceforward one Consul must always be a Plebeian (though there was no rule that the other must be a Patrician); Plebeians were eligible for all magistracies, and for seats in the Senate. The whole body of the Plebs met in a new sort of public assembly from which Patricians were excluded; this *Consilium Plebis* passed laws which were binding on the whole community. The Plebeians elected certain officials called *Tribunes* who represented the interests of the non-Patrician citizen. Although these Tribunes did not rank as magistrates and did not hold the Imperium, or power to give orders, any Tribune might countermand the orders of even the highest magistrates, and in other ways interpose his veto in behalf of the Plebeian.

The Roman constitution now gave supreme and undivided power to the following: a Dictator (rarely), a Censor (intermittently), two Consuls and eight Prætors (all the time). In addition there were the ten Tribunes,

who themselves could do nothing, but who each sep-
arately, at his own whim, could prevent anything being
done. Obviously such a state could be expected to ex-
plode from mere internal stress.

Instead of which the invincible City grew ever
stronger. The Plebs elected reasonable Tribunes, who
remedied individual cases of injustice but did not interfere with general decisions. The Patricians welcomed into
the Senate educated Plebeians with a good military
record. The Roman citizen—Plebeian and Patrician,
elector and magistrate—seemed dedicated to maintaining, in spite of the potential weaknesses of the constitution, the harmony of the Roman State.

Another reason why Rome grew strong was that she
treated her allies and conquered subjects with generosity.
An Italian city conquered by Rome had something to
hope for. The tribute was light, and if the contingent
fought faithfully there was the hope of citizenship. Re-
lations with each city were governed by a separate treaty,
but in general one may say that faithful and Italian-
speaking cities were rewarded with Roman citizenship
for every citizen, after a period of probation.

The result was displayed in the great Punic Wars
(264–147 B.C.) when Rome, already the leading state
in Italy, came into collision with Carthage, the Semitic
trading city which ruled the coasts of north Africa and
Spain. In 217 B.C. Hannibal, the great Carthaginian
leader, invaded Italy and overthrew the main Rome field
armies one after another. Then he set out to raise rebel-

lion among the subject cities of Italy—and the outlying
subjects of Rome fought gallantly for their overlord.

In the course of these wars Rome conquered Mace-
donia, the seaboard of Spain, and much of Asia Minor;
though it was the Roman custom to leave civilized states
in formal independence, as Romans were diffident about
ruling those whom they considered more cultured than
themselves.

The Senate, meeting every day, negotiated with foreign envoys, prepared treaties, and supervised the operations of the many armies simultaneously in the field
against the Carthaginians, drawing up instruction for
each general. In other words, what had once been a
body of councilors was fast becoming the executive government.

The Romans had now attained to what many think-
ers consider the best form of government, administration
by the most eminent men in the state, appointed for life
and so not tempted to vote-catching demagogy; but with
all vital questions, declarations of war or important
changes in the law, submitted to the judgment of uni-
versal suffrage in the Comitia. At the outset of his career
each Senator had won election to a magistracy, which
kept out the wellborn halfwit or the unpopular eccentric.
The unstated axiom of the republic was no longer that
any Roman citizen was capable of filling any position,
but that every Senator was equally capable of responsible
command, and that the plums of office should be passed
round fairly.

There was growing up another unstated axiom, that the son of a Senator had a moral right to step into his father's shoes. Even in the untrammeled democracy of the United States men named Roosevelt, Taft, or La Follette seem to be elected to office more often than the blind laws of chance would indicate; in Rome a candidate who came before the Comitia with the backing of a united Senate stood a very good chance of election; and such people were usually the promising sons of serving Senators. The result was the emergence of a new aristocracy, having nothing in common with the old Patricians.

This equilibrium depended on a feeling of rough equality among all the three hundred Senators, and on a sense among politicians that it was unsporting and possibly dangerous to push an advantage to the limit and triumph utterly over defeated opponents. Two things might overthrow it: the emergence of a popular leader too eminent to fit into the system of fair shares for all Senators, or the appearance of an organized political party out to get everything the law allowed to its adherents. In 134 B.C., a generation before the birth of Cæsar, both came at once.

In that year Tiberius Sempronius Gracchus was elected Tribune, on a program of dividing conquered land among the people, especially those people who had the good sense to vote for Gracchus. This public land was largely occupied by wealthy Senators who had granted it to themselves at a nominal rent; and after the long wars Rome was full of ex-soldiers who had been raised on a farm and clamored for a veterans' bonus in the form of a free holding. But the public land was an essential war-reserve, which in a crisis might be sold to equip an army; it was improvident to distribute it gratis among the voters in time of peace.

It was the kind of conflict of interests which the Romans were expert in resolving by peaceful means. Some compromise would have emerged after years of bargaining. But Gracchus had been reading Greek political theory, and he conceived of Rome as a democracy in which all power resided in the Comitia; he was also in a hurry. The Senate, quite legally, persuaded another Tribune to veto the proposed Agrarian Law. Gracchus carried in the Comitia a motion deposing Octavius, the Tribune who dared to thwart the will of the people. After argument Octavius withdrew, in fear of his life, and the Agrarian Law was carried by tumultuous acclamation.

Gracchus had exposed an ambiguity at the heart of the Roman constitution, an ambiguity which was only resolved when Augustus, the heir of Cæsar, finally destroyed liberty in the name of the people. In any constitution of checks and balances one power must be sovereign in the last resort; the Romans had never made up their minds whether this ultimate sovereignty lay in the Comitia, where every citizen might vote, or in the Senate, that great reserve of experienced political wisdom. But Gracchus had chosen to fight on very unfavorable ground. He had weakened the office of Tribune, the office he himself held; and he had offended

Roman sentiment, which felt very strongly that the in-violability of even unpopular and wrongheaded Trib-unes was the chief guarantee of personal liberty.

The Senators were careful to keep within the law. Since the Comitia had spoken, the division of public lands began. But Tribunes were elected for one year only, and consecutive re-election was forbidden; though the same man might be Tribune more than once, there must be an interval when, as a private citizen, he could be prosecuted for illegalities committed in office. It was now June, and Gracchus must retire in December; in half a year the division of lands would not get very far, and the best lawyers in the Senate were conferring to bring a really deadly prosecution against their chief op-ponent.

Recklessly, Gracchus again broke the fundamental law; he announced that he would run for immediate re-election. If you granted his premise, that the Comitia could do anything, as the British House of Commons can do anything, then obviously the Comitia might elect anyone to the Tribunate; but in that case a popular leader might be inviolable and unprosecuted until he died of old age.

The election for next year's Tribunes took place in July. Gracchus ran, as he had threatened; and the Sena-tors at first tried to prevent his re-election by putting up another Tribune to veto it. After several days of squab-bling over procedure, the popular party had its way and Gracchus was declared elected. The laws had been defied with impunity, and the Senators saw that nothing was left but the sword. Publius Scipio Nasica, an ex-Consul, led into the Forum a group of Senators and their adherents, armed with clubs broken from the benches of the Senate House itself. In the fighting which followed, Gracchus and three hundred of his party were slain, and the constitution was saved.

But blood had been shed in the Forum; the civil wars had begun. Henceforth the body of Roman citizens was divided into the Populars, who revered the memory of Gracchus, and the Optimates, who followed the Senate. I shall use these names throughout this book; though we must remember that the Populars were not the people of Rome, but that minority of the people who were full citizens; and that the Optimates were not the best men except in the sense that they belonged to good families. But in America Democrats believe in a republican form of government, and Republicans advocate democracy. It is always prudent to refer to parties by the names they themselves have chosen.

Ten years later Caius Sempronius Gracchus, the younger brother of Tiberius, was elected Tribune on a program almost entirely of naked revenge. To win support he also proposed a wide extension of Roman citizenship among the Italians, and the foundation of colonies of citizens who should be granted free houses and farms where the strategic situation called for permanent Roman garrisons. Political parties can never be brought to admit that any part of their past program was mistaken, and for the future the idea of extended franchise and the foundation of colonies became part of the mental equipment of the Populars; though it had nothing to do with the real cause of quarrel, the rights of the Senate.

While his brother had been willing to fight only if his proposals could not be carried peacefully, Caius Gracchus was eager for civil war. He went about with an armed bodyguard of party members, and in general dared the Senate to defend itself. In the year 121 his supporters, having lost the elections, attempted to murder one of the newly chosen Consuls, Lucius Opimius. The Senate then passed the Ultimate Decree, a declaration that the magistrates must restore order at all costs; Optimates claimed that this gave the Consuls power to execute citizens without trial, but the Populars denied it; and this was the chief constitutional ground of party strife. Caius Gracchus seized and fortified the temple of Diana, while the Optimates assembled in arms at the temple of Castor and Pollux; a regular battle was fought all over the Forum and the neighboring streets; the Optimates were victorious, and Caius Gracchus was killed in the rout.

It will be noted that when it came to fighting, the three hundred Senators, with their followers, could overcome the Populars, who in theory were the whole body of citizens assembled in Comitia. This shows that the transient majority in the Comitia no longer represented the citizens as a whole. A Roman could vote only by coming down to the Forum in person; that ruled out the very large number of citizens who by this period lived at a distance from Rome; often it ruled out all the country farmers, though for great occasions, such as the annual

Consular elections, numbers of farmers came specially to the City; in fact anyone who was busy earning his own living could not regularly attend the daily Comitia. But ancient city-states provided relief for citizens in want, and it had become the custom to grant a daily ration of corn to any citizen who could show that he was without means. It was these idle corner-boys, with time on their hands, who provided the daily majority in the Comitia. If left to themselves they voted for Popular candidates, as the Populars stood for bigger and better out-relief; but they were easily bribed, and the Optimates had the money to bribe them.

One tiresome result of this state of affairs was that often neither faction won a clear-cut victory in the elections. The two Consuls might represent opposite parties, and among the Tribunes were always some servants of the Senate. That made difficulties for the administration.

But a much more sinister result was that it was now possible to appeal from a chance vote of the unrepresentative Comitia to the great body of right-thinking men who had been too busy to attend; and the only way these right-thinking men could prove the strength of their opinions was with their swords.

After the death of Caius Gracchus the Optimates governed Rome for thirteen years. They had a coherent and reasonable political philosophy, and knew that their system of rule entailed certain disadvantages; they were willing to pay a price for what they considered the most valuable gift of a good constitution, personal liberty. Sparta had sacrificed liberty to gain military efficiency;

Athens had placed the life and fortune of every citizen
at the mercy of an ephemeral majority in the popular
Assembly; the Optimates of Rome knew that strong
government is always tyrannical government, and they
deliberately arranged that supreme power should pass, at
very short intervals, from one corrupt and incompetent
nobleman to another. The Consuls so chosen were often
bad generals, who retired with a fortune after one year of
unsalaried service to the State. But military genius was
not looked for in a Consul. It was his business to bring
his army into contact with the enemy; then the soldier's
broadsword would gain victory in hand-to-hand conflict,
without the deceptive glamour of brilliant strategy. As to
peculation by the high command, the Republic could
afford the slight expense. Roman citizens paid no taxes
at all, except a small subscription for the purchase of
sacrificial beasts (so that every citizen should share in
the state sacrifices). The revenue of the City was entirely made up of plunder taken in war or the tribute of
subject-allies. If the Consuls were greedy, that only
meant that more wars must be fought and more plunder
taken from the foe.

A party machine, on principle without a supreme
leader, was in control of the elections. Consuls so chosen
would not dare to interfere with the liberty either of
elderly statesmen who had been Consuls in the past or
of young nobles who might be Consuls in the future.
Above all, the machine had no liking for a brilliant
leader, who might become so popular with the electorate
that he could overthrow the constitution. But liberty

was safe, and the people in general were content so long as no exterior danger threatened defeat in war.

An aristocracy can continue to govern only if it is willing to open its ranks to any newcomer of sufficient genius. The Roman Senate was suddenly faced with a great soldier of low birth; most unwisely the nobles mocked his uncouth manners and drove him into the arms of the Populars. The gain of the Populars thereby was more than they then knew, for this soldier was not only great in his own right but he was also to become the uncle of Caius Julius Cæsar.

Caius Marius was born on a poor farm in 159 B.C. and began work as a laborer; he joined the army as a common soldier, and rose by sheer merit to the high rank of Military Tribune (say Brigadier General). In 119 he was elected Tribune, and signalized his arrival in the front rank of politics by marrying Julia, a lady of most distinguished family, sister of Caius Julius Cæsar, Patrician and ex-Prætor and father of the future Imperator. In 115 he was himself elected Prætor, which was as far as the Optimates thought such a man should go. But an unimportant colonial war in Africa was being badly managed by a succession of noble Consuls; when Marius stood for the Consulship of 107 he was easily elected, against the whole weight of the official machine.

Marius was an inspired trainer of troops. He made important alterations in the drill of the Roman army, all in the direction of using a few highly trained men to hold a front that had previously been held by close-packed but half-trained militia; that widened the gulf between

the citizen who had performed his military service and
the idler in the Forum who had never been drafted. In
addition he made two changes in the administration of
the army which had enduring consequences in the
history of the whole world: first, he increased the soldier's pay, so that service in the army became a profitable
career, instead of a tiresome and unwillingly endured
interruption of work on the farm; secondly, he raised
his men, not by the customary selective draft, but by
calling for volunteers, with the implied promise that
they would serve only under his command. Henceforth
the Roman soldier was a professional, enlisted for twenty
years with the option of re-engagement; and he joined
to follow a particular general, taking an oath to be faithful to this general instead of the old oath to obey the
magistrates of the Republic.

As Consul, Marius went to Africa and soon cleaned
up the revolt of Jugurtha. By this time it had been realized that one year's tenure of command was too short for
any general to finish a campaign, and the custom had
grown up of prolonging overseas commands by extending the term of a Consul or Prætor; he then commanded
as pro-Consul or pro-Prætor, with all his original powers.
But these powers automatically expired if he entered the
city of Rome, for that proved either that he was neg-
lecting his duty or that the campaign was finished.

Marius remained in Africa as pro-Consul, winding up
the rebellion, until he was suddenly called home by an
unexpected menace to Italy. This was the first appearance of the Germans on the Roman horizon.

We must remember that the Roman army had nothing, except discipline, that barbarian hosts could not match; a German sword was just as sharp as a Roman one. The Romans had in the end conquered the barbarian Gauls who lived between the Alps and the river Po; but that was because Romans obeyed orders, while a Gallic chief never knew whether his tribesmen would follow when he led them against the foe. Now two southern German tribes, the Cimbri and Teutones, bigger and fiercer men than any Gaul, having devastated the Roman province on the Mediterranean coast of modern France, were poised before the western passes into Italy.

Rome was in a panic. The populace insisted on placing command in the hands of the best general, though it was most emphatically not his turn for another year of office. Marius was made Consul for 104, though he was in Africa when the elections were held, and could not canvass in person. This was the first time any man had been elected in his absence, and such reliance on one savior was an evil omen for the continuance of the aristocratic Republic.

Marius destroyed the German invaders so completely that these particular tribes never bothered the Romans again. The campaign finished in the year 101, and he returned to Rome to celebrate his Triumph, the grand procession terminating in a religious service (with traces of the original rite of human sacrifice) that was granted to a victorious Consul or Prætor only by a special decree of the Senate. But during the war he had been repeatedly elected to the Consulship; his first term, in 107, had been followed by a short but decent interval; but in 104, 103, 102, 101, and 100 he was continually Consul. For four hundred years no Roman had held such personal power. The constitution, first breached by Tiberius Gracchus, was now in dissolution.

In July 100, when his aunt's husband Marius was Consul for the sixth time, Caius Julius Cæsar was born.

CHAPTER THREE
CÆSAR'S EARLY LIFE

EVERY Roman citizen had three names, though sometimes the third was never used in documents and has not
come down to us. The system is often misunderstood,
and should be explained fully. The *gentile*, or clan
name, was the name par excellence, which proved that
its bearer was a citizen; it came second. In the case of
Caius Julius Cæsar the clan name marked him as a
member of the *gens* Julia. Cæsar, which means "bushy
hair," had been given to some ancestral Julius to distinguish him from other members of the clan. But these
cognomens, or after-names, had long ago lost their literal
significance; no one expected Cæsar to have a lot of hair.
The cognomen was in the first place inherited from the
father; but it still kept some flavor of the nickname from
which it had originated. It might be changed by a solemn
decree of the appropriate authorities; and sometimes a
man would quietly drop his undistinguished cognomen
without anyone's permission, as Cæsar's great-nephew
Augustus dropped Thuricus, the cognomen of his father.

The chief purpose of the *prænomen*, or fore-name,
was to distinguish a man from his brothers. As Cæsar was
an only son, probably no one ever called him Caius except his mother while he was a baby. In legal docu-

ments he would be Caius Julius Cæsar, and in common speech Cæsar alone. But after his successor took to calling himself Cæsar Augustus, posterity referred to him as Julius Cæsar, a combination seldom used in his lifetime.

By the way, females were known only by their gentile names. Cæsar's only daughter was called simply Julia, and if he had had ten daughters the tenth would have been Julia Decima. It must have been confusing in the nursery.

The Romans, remembering their mixed origin, were without excessive pride of race; they had no color-bar, and granted citizenship liberally to foreigners. But each individual Roman was extremely proud of his own ancestors. In early times they had practiced formal ancestor-worship, and in Cæsar's day it was still customary to commemorate all dead ancestors on the occasion of every funeral in the family. In the funeral procession every ancestor who had been a magistrate was impersonated by a living actor, dressed in the official robes to which he had been entitled, and wearing a mask modeled on his features. Busts of the illustrious dead were kept in an honored shrine beside the household gods in the chief reception room of every great house.

On his father's side young Caius was descended from Romulus, the founder of the City, and so ultimately from Æneas, who fled from Troy to Italy; as Æneas was a son of the goddess Venus, the whole *gens* Julia might claim divine ancestry. In the female line he was descended from Ancus Martius, an ancient king of Rome. He was therefore a Patrician, though by this date the distinction was important only in religious matters; as a Patrician he could not be elected Tribune, but he would be welcomed into any of the Colleges of Pontiffs who managed the ceremonial of the state religion.

In later times stories grew up of the omens that had attended his birth; he was also supposed to be singled out from other men as the first baby to be born by Cæsarean section. If that is true, it was a most successful operation; both mother and child survived without blemish, and his mother lived on for many years after. But he had no brothers, and only two sisters.

His father, also named Caius Julius Cæsar, was distinguished only by his noble descent. He became Prætor, but never Consul; in fact, for six generations the family had not gone beyond the Prætorship. They were not notably rich, and though in their hall they kept a long line of busts, the noble ancestors who would swell the funeral procession of every Julius, these ancestors were more numerous than famous.

But of course Caius had one great asset. His uncle by marriage was Marius, the great general who now held the Consulship for the sixth time, and who could make himself ruler of the City if he had a mind to it.

Unfortunately Marius was an incompetent politician. He was the natural leader of the Populars, who at this time were campaigning for more free land (their perpetual war cry), and for the extension of Roman citizenship to all Italians. If Marius had been willing to overthrow the Republic he could have made himself monarch with Popular support; or if he had shown

himself a respecter of the forms of the constitution the
Senate might in the end have become reconciled to his
low origin and uncouth manners.

The Populars, as had become their habit, relied on
riotous intimidation to get their proposals through the
Comitia. In the summer of 100, when the elections were
held for the year 99 B.C., they murdered Memmius, the
leading candidate of the Optimates. The Senators then
gathered their armed retainers while the two Popular
leaders, Saturninus and Glaucia, barricaded themselves
in the Capitol, the old citadel; where they proclaimed
a complete social revolution, including freedom for all
slaves and citizenship for everybody.

Since Marius, as Consul, was in charge of the preser-
vation of order, he might have led either side to victory.
Instead he dithered. In his heart he wished for a Popular victory, but he was hampered by his inborn respect
for the constitution. The Senate commissioned him to
assault the Capitol, and after some havering he regret-
fully complied. Saturninus and Glaucia surrendered un-
conditionally, and were imprisoned pending trial. But a
crowd of young Optimates broke into the prison and
lynched them; which was sacrilege as well as murder,
for Saturninus was an inviolable Tribune. Marius had
now made himself distrusted by both sides. In December, when his sixth Consulship expired, he set off on a
long tour of the oracles of Asia, a dignified form of
voluntary exile. But long ago a witch had told him that
he would be Consul seven times, and he believed the
prophecy. The politicians thought the stupid old gen-

eral could be written off as a political failure; Marius himself was certain that one day he would come back.

So when young Caius was in his nursery his family lived very quietly; his father, brother-in-law to the unsuccessful would-be tyrant, was in mild disgrace, and if he had taken a prominent part in politics his head would have been in danger. With his mother's milk the child would suck up two prejudices: that Optimates were nasty people, who oppressed the *gens* Julia; and that politics was a dangerous business in which death was often the penalty of failure.

Meanwhile the victorious Optimates were governing with their usual incompetence. It was the old Roman tradition to be generous in extending the citizenship; but the Populars had proposed to enfranchise all Italy, and any loyal party man sees at once that the proposals of the opposition must be wrong. The Optimates decided that there were enough Roman citizens already; there were nearly half a million of them, scattered all over the Mediterranean.

The Italians, who did not follow Roman politics closely, knew only that the last administration had promised to enfranchise them, and that now the promise was being broken. At length their patience was exhausted, and in the year 91 began the War against the Allies (the Social War), one of the sternest struggles in which Rome was ever engaged.

The City itself might have fallen to the enemy, for this was a war against the sturdy peasants who formed the backbone of the legions, men who displayed just as much discipline and devotion to duty as the Romans themselves. But a general of genius appeared to give Rome the victory, and then as usual the victorious general of genius found himself too big for the constitution.

Lucius Cornelius Sulla, an aristocrat from one of the noblest Senatorial families, had been Quæstor to Marius in the African campaign; he had personally captured the rebel king Jugurtha, by treachery certainly, but at great risk to his own life. The Populars hated him, and he hated them; but he had been elected Consul for 88 to win the war, and he had won it. Earlier Marius had returned to lead an army against the Allies; which the more bitter Populars regarded as a betrayal of his own side. Now King Mithridates of Pontus, of whom more later, had invaded the Roman possessions in Asia and a great army must be sent against him. Should its leader be Marius the old Popular or Sulla the young Optimate? The Populars decided to get their man in by their usual violent methods. The election was so disorderly that the two Consuls, Quintus Pompeius Rufus and Sulla, adjourned it indefinitely. Then the Populars poured into the street, drove both Consuls into hiding, and declared carried their whole party program.

Sulla took refuge with his army, which was besieging Nola, the last stronghold of the Italian rebels. His troops proved loyal to him, and he led them straight to Rome; for the first time a Roman general led his men across the sacred Pomœrium, where every citizen should lay aside his arms. Although Marius took command of the Populars, proclaiming cancellation of all debts and freedom for all slaves, Sulla got in after a mere skirmish. Marius fled, and the heads of other Popular leaders were nailed up in the Forum. Rome was nakedly under the rule of the sword.

But Sulla was not particularly interested in governing Rome. He was eager to get to Asia, where King Mithridates of Pontus, a descendant of the ancient Persian royal house, was leading a coalition of native Asiatics and Greek cities against the new and barbarous power from the west. After a few summary executions Sulla held the delayed Consular elections. Even though these ended in a draw, with the election of Cnæus Octavius, an Optimate, and Lucius Cornelius Cinna, a Popular, he then led his army to the east.

The year 87, the last year of Cæsar's childhood (for Roman Patricians came legally of age at fourteen), was the worst period of anarchy the City had yet experienced. The two Consuls assumed office in January, and at once embarked on a regular civil war, which left ten thousand dead in the streets of Rome. For the first time the Populars were successful in the fight. Old Marius, who had been hiding in Africa, reappeared in Italy at the head of an army of brigands and freed slaves; the Optimates surrendered, and with this ragged force he occupied Rome. The Consul Octavius was hacked to death while wearing his official robes and seated on his official throne. Many other Optimates were murdered, and the wife and children of Sulla barely escaped into penniless exile.

Among the victims was Cnæus Cornelius Merula,

the *Flamen Dialis*, or High Priest of Jupiter; because he had arranged the peaceful surrender of Rome, he was allowed to commit suicide, avoiding the disgrace of death at the hands of the public executioner. His office was one of those restricted to Patricians, and the Populars were short of Patrician supporters; casting round for someone to fill it, Marius recalled the young nephew of his wife; at the age of thirteen Caius was made Flamen, a sinecure whose purely ceremonial duties might be performed by deputy. But he was now marked out, through no fault of his own, as a supporter of the bloodiest and least scrupulous wing of the Popular party.

In January the witch's prophecy was fulfilled; Marius could enjoy his seventh Consulship (far more than any man had held before him). But in the same month he died, at the age of seventy-three. Cinna, who had retained his Consulship without the formality of another election, appointed a Popular, Lucius Valerius Flaccus, to fill the vacancy, and then sent him off to Asia with orders to arrest Sulla and assume command in the war against Mithridates. For two years the Populars were supreme in Rome. They did not so much change the laws as rule without regard to them. They reduced every debt by three quarters, and were generous with the corn dole; but otherwise they had no program, except to take the property of Optimates and add it to their own.

Meanwhile Sulla, though technically outlawed and deprived of his command, devoted all his attention to the war against Mithridates. When the unfortunate Flaccus reached Asia he was murdered by his own men,

who either joined Sulla or set up as brigands. In 84
Sulla wrote to the Senate to announce that he was nego-
tiating peace with the defeated Mithridates and would
come home to restore order as soon as he was at leisure.
Cinna recruited an army to fight him, but when he ordered his men to march they lynched him instead. The
remaining Populars intensified the reign of terror, but
were unable to raise an army capable of meeting Sulla in
the field. In 83 Sulla landed in Italy; the cities of the
south, strongly Popular in sympathy, held him up for a
year; but in 82 he entered Rome, destroyed the last
army of the Italian rebels, and found himself supreme.
Both Consuls-elect for 81 had been killed in the fighting, and following the strict letter of the constitution an
Interrex was appointed, whose task was to nominate a
Dictator within three days or himself resign and desig-
nate another Interrex. Of course the only possible choice
for Dictator was Sulla. He accepted the office, announcing that he would hold it, not for six months, but
for as long as, in his own opinion, he was needed.

Cæsar was now eighteen, a tall slender youth with
handsome features and rather more charm and frivolity
than were considered fitting in a Roman aristocrat. There
are no anecdotes about his childhood; wealthy Roman
boys did not go to school, but were taught by private
tutors; as a result the companions of their infancy were
usually obscure slaves. None the less, this absence of
anecdotes indicates that Cæsar did not make any particular mark in his early youth.

But even at eighteen he was not afraid of taking his

own line and facing the consequences of a dangerous gamble. He was by marriage the nephew of Marius, which was dangerous now that Sulla had seized power; but the *gens* Julia was not as a whole committed to the disgraced Popular faction; in fact two of its members, Lucius and another Caius Cæsar, had been among the Optimates murdered by Marius in 87. Cæsar might quietly have joined the victorious Senatorial party, and in fact it would be the natural thing for the young head of a Patrician house to do. (His father had died three years before.)

Instead he went out of his way to emphasize his connection with the proscribed opposition. He had been betrothed in infancy, after the usual Roman fashion, to a little girl of suitable birth and sufficient dowry; but in 83 he broke off the engagement, to marry, against the wishes of his family, the daughter of the lately murdered Cinna (her only name, as explained above, was Cornelia). Such a marriage at such a time could only be inspired by genuine love. In after life Cæsar was notorious for promiscuous attachments, and he could never be considered a model husband; but he was capable of deep affection for a woman (which most Romans were not), and this was not the only occasion on which romantic love, that rarity in the ancient world, endangered his career.

The devouring ambition which was the mainspring of his life may also have influenced his choice of a partner. The leading Populars were all dead or in exile, but they still had supporters. The leaderless party would note

that one intelligent young man of excellent family remained faithful to the old cause.

Sulla ruled more or less within the law, as his aim was
to restore the constitution as it had been before the rise
of Tiberius Gracchus. But he used his power as Dictator
to outlaw those members of the opposition who might
have caused trouble. Lists were posted in the Forum,
and if a man's name was on the list ("proscribed") it
meant that all his property was forfeit and that a reward
was offered for his head.

At eighteen Cæsar was not important enough to merit
proscription, in spite of his regrettable family connections. But of course Sulla was aware of his existence, for
the few hundred Senatorial families formed a small and
exclusive society. The young man was not to blame
for the indiscretions of his aunt, but he had shown im-
pudence in marrying the daughter of a dangerous revolutionary; and that the revolutionary was dead at the
time of the marriage removed even the excuse that he
was seeking an influential father-in-law. Sulla summoned
the boy before him and spoke to him severely. He was
then dismissed unharmed, with orders to divorce Cornelia and find a more suitable bride. (Roman law permitted divorce at will, though of course only at the will
of the husband.)

Cæsar refused, partly because he loved Cornelia, but
partly from the dislike of being ordered about by a fellow citizen which was the most deeply ingrained trait
in every Roman. It was an astonishingly brave thing to
do, for at that time Sulla held untrammeled power of

life and death. To have a chance of escape if he were proscribed, Cæsar then went into hiding among the Sabine mountaineers, who had been staunch allies of the defeated Populars.

Under a tyranny, to go into hiding is itself a confession of guilt. Cornelius Phagito, commander of a band of soldiers detached to search the Sabine hills for outlaws, discovered him in a peasant's hut. Phagito knew that if he reported his discovery he would receive the usual reward; but no Roman liked to be known as an informer, and he had nothing personally against the young man. He preferred blackmail, and took a large bribe to keep his mouth shut. If he had decided the other way, the world at this moment would be a different place.

Meanwhile Cæsar, though on the run, had never been technically outlawed. His very high birth, which had drawn down the wrath of Sulla on a boy with no political record, carried some compensating advantages; his respectable relatives went into action. Lucius Aurelius Cotta, his mother's brother, headed a distinguished delegation to seek pardon for this eminent young noble. Sulla favored eminent young nobles as a class, and the boy had done nothing dangerous. But at his first interview Sulla had been impressed by Cæsar's personality; he allowed himself to be persuaded, but he was impelled to prophesy. "You may have his life," he exclaimed. "Only bear in mind that one day this man may destroy the cause that you and I uphold. For this Cæsar is worth six of Marius."

Sulla was genuinely anxious to restore the old constitution, which he considered would work excellently after a few minor alterations. He passed a series of laws giving to the Senate all the powers previously in dispute, such as the right to enact the Ultimate Decree and to draw up the agenda for the Comitia; by a stroke of remarkable ingenuity he destroyed the power of the Tribunes without in any way infringing their inviolable rights; he merely decreed that a citizen who had served as Tribune was incapable of holding any other office. The real influence of the Tribunate depended on the courage and independence of the individual Tribune; now no man of courage and independence would seek election to a post which ended his political career.

Sulla might have made himself king, but he preferred to remain a Roman noble. In the year 79 he presided over the normal Consular elections, and then, before the Comitia could disperse, announced his resignation. Dismissing his Lictors, he asked from the speaker's platform whether any citizen wished to prosecute Lucius Cornelius Sulla, a private citizen, for misdeeds committed while he held the office of Dictator. There was no reply, and the great man strolled off unattended to his private house. He had made many enemies, but the Romans were so delighted at this unexpected restoration of their freedom that they allowed him to live unmolested; until in 78 he died of drink and debauchery, respected by all.

Cæsar at the age of eighteen undertook the period of military service which was an essential preliminary to a political career. Although he was of Senatorial family

and would probably in due course become a Senator, he
was as yet only a knight. He was appointed to the staff
of Marcus Minutius Thermus, Sulla's legate in Asia and
presumably a friend of the family. (A legate was not an
elected magistrate; he was the deputy of a magistrate,
who appointed him on his own responsibility.) Cæsar
left his young wife in Rome, as was the usual custom.

Sulla had made a truce with King Mithridates of
Pontus because he was anxious to get back to Rome and
finish off the Populars. The war broke out again, like
so many unnecessary Roman frontier wars, because an
ambitious provincial governor wanted to earn the Triumph which was the reward of victory. Mithridates did
not wish to fight, but Lucius Licinius Murena, pro-
Prætor of Asia, badgered him into revolt. Murena soon
got all the war he wanted, for Mithridates defeated him
in a pitched battle. Then Sulla, who dared not leave
Rome, patched up a truce at long range. The war was
quickly over, save that the Greek city of Mytilene,
which had declared for Mithridates, remained in hope-
less and isolated resistance.

In this unimportant war, which settled nothing and
whose chronology is obscure, Cæsar first saw action.
During the siege of Mytilene he won the Civic Crown,
a decoration granted for saving the life of a fellow citizen in the face of the enemy. Oddly enough, we know
nothing of the circumstances, not even the name of the
soldier whose life he saved. But for the rest of his life
Cæsar's courage could never be doubted; for though
the crown itself was worn only once, on the day it was

granted, the recipient bore ever after a small badge which fulfilled the purpose of our modern medal-ribbons. Yet courage was a quality taken for granted in a young Roman noble. Cæsar had been lucky to win official recognition during his first campaign, but he did not stand out among his brave contemporaries.

His other exploit during this war was of a very different stamp. It betrayed his only weakness, a lack of sympathy with his fellow citizens which sometimes led him to outrage public opinion through sheer ignorance of the manner in which his actions would strike his contemporaries. Cæsar was a lonely man, as all his actions show, and his own broad-minded indifference to precedent sometimes led him astray.

During the siege Murena needed a fleet, and King Nicomedes of Bithynia, a subject-ally of Rome, had one. Like the other chieftains of Asia, Nicomedes was hesitating whether to support Mithridates or to stay loyal, and young Cæsar was sent to confirm him in his duty. The King, delighted to prove his own importance, made conditions; he would lend his fleet if the handsome young Roman noble would sleep with him. Without a second thought Cæsar complied. The Bithynian fleet blockaded Mytilene, which presently surrendered, and Cæsar could feel that he had done his country valuable service.

Now the ancient Greeks, because they kept their women in seclusion, frequently embarked on love-affairs with boys; for it is impossible to woo a secluded lady, yet courtship is half the pleasure of love. For the same reason homosexuality is common nowadays in

Moslem lands where the harem system prevails. The primitive Romans had been virile enough, but when they took up Greek culture they also adopted Greek vices. By the first century B.C. Greek customs were so established in Rome that no one would frown on genuine love between males. Yet even the most enthusiastic practitioner of unnatural vice feels a certain contempt for the passive partner, and if the passive partner submits only for profit, against his inclination, that contempt is very deep indeed. By defiling himself to please King Nicomedes, Cæsar had sunk to the level of a male prostitute, forgetting the dignity due to a Roman and a Patrician. Every Roman who heard the story was shocked; the memory of King Nicomedes stuck to Cæsar's reputation like a bur, and was resurrected every time an opponent made a speech attacking him.

So long as Sulla lived, Cæsar thought it wise to remain in Asia, out of the way. In 78 he was serving on the staff of Publius Servilius, pro-Consul in Cilicia, who was continuing the unending war against the pirates of those parts. But as soon as the retired Dictator was dead he thought it safe to come home, to commence the political career that was normal for one of his birth. He was nearly twenty-two, which was rather late to begin.

CHAPTER FOUR

THE RISING POLITICIAN

THE PEACE of Sulla died with its maker, and Cæsar found Rome enduring a full-scale civil war. The elections of 79 had ended in a draw, with the two Consuls for 78 representing opposite parties. A minor rebellion in Etruria gave the Popular Consul, Marcus Æmilius Lepidus, an excuse to gather an army to crush it. As soon as he was at large with a body of troops behind him he made war on the Optimate Consul, Quintus Lutatius Catulus. Neither Consul was a particularly skillful soldier, but the Optimates were still the stronger party; in a battle near Rome Lepidus was beaten, and though he escaped to Sardinia he soon died there. Two groups of Populars remained in arms; Quintus Sertorius had defeated or won over the Roman garrison of Spain, and with the support of the native Spaniards held the whole peninsula for the cause of Marius and the citizenship for all civilized men; he was a competent general and a magnificent colonial governor, and it was several years before his revolt was stamped out. In Italy Marcus Junius Brutus held the strong walls of Modena with an isolated detachment from the army of Lepidus. He had no prospect of relief, but he had no hope of mercy; and he endured to the bitter end. His widow, Servilia, had been Cæsar's mistress, and fashionable gossip made Cæsar the father of her infant son. I myself cannot see how this could have come about, unless Servilia visited Asia in 79. But that was undoubtedly what people said at the time.

The government of Optimates could still keep its end up in the everlasting civil war, which had never completely died out since the killing of Tiberius Gracchus. But it was singularly incompetent, even for an aristocratic government, and though it might overcome its open enemies it was at the mercy of overweening friends. Cnæus Pompeius had proved himself an efficient commander under Sulla; in 82 he had been sent to defeat the Populars of Sicily as legate for the Dictator, and had brilliantly carried out his mission. He had then betrayed the harmless but irritating vanity which guided all his life by asking to be granted the cognomen of Magnus by solemn legal decree. It was contrary to etiquette to grant an honorary cognomen to a mere legate, who had never been elected by the people to a magistracy; but Cnæus Pompeius Magnus had his way. In 78 he bullied the Senate into giving him a command in Italy against Lepidus, and in 77 he was granted far-reaching powers to fight Sertorius in Spain; all without the conventional preliminary of election. Pompeius knew the intricacies of the Roman constitution, and in his fashion he respected it; but he always sought to be granted exceptions personal to himself, usually mere titular distinctions which irritated his rivals without increasing his own power. What he really desired in his heart was to be absolute ruler of a free Republic, a contradiction that in the end brought him to a squalid death. But in 77, at the age of twenty-nine, he was the Senate's indispensable general and, though still without elective office, one of the first men in the state. Cæsar, aged twenty-three, was quite undistinguished; if he was known at all it was as the nephew by marriage of Marius, and the protagonist in a funny but dirty story about the goings-on of Asiatic kings.

Cæsar decided to make himself known to the electorate by conducting a political prosecution, a method of self-advertisement sometimes practiced by ambitious office-seekers of the present day. In classical Rome it had the excuse of being the only way to convict a political evildoer. There was no paid State Attorney whose duty it was to enforce the law; and both the letter of the constitution and, still more binding, the climate of public opinion insisted that every advocate must come into court as an unpaid volunteer. (By an echo of this rule English barristers may not sue for their fees, which in theory are the free-will offerings of grateful clients.) In Rome that was fact as well as theory. Advocacy was not a skilled profession entered by examination; all citizens did in fact know the law, and a citizen in trouble either conducted his own case or persuaded a more distinguished citizen to speak for him, purely as a favor.

Cæsar, remembering that he was by descent and by marriage a hereditary leader of the Populars, prosecuted for extortion two moderately well-known provincial governors, Cnæus Cornelius Dolabella and Caius Antonius Hybrida, both veterans of the Sullan faction. The tribunal before which he pleaded was a commission of more than a hundred middle-class citizens, chosen with a high property-qualification; this commission is often called a jury, but its numbers made it more like a public meeting, and it was swayed by eloquence rather than evidence. Cæsar was a very good speaker, but both the accused were acquitted. The acquittal was probably as political in motive as the prosecution; Sertorius was doing far too well in Spain, and the well-to-do commission, fearing a Popular revival, determined to support all veteran Optimates without bothering about their crimes.

Cæsar saw that the prevailing prejudice against his Popular connections ruled out all hope of a career for the present. His wisest course was to retire from Rome until opinion changed. He set off for the prosperous Greek island of Rhodes, to study rhetoric under the famous Apollonius Molo, who at one time or another taught Cicero and every famous orator of that generation.

During his stay in the east he suffered a very celebrated adventure. While crossing from Miletus to Rhodes he was captured by pirates. Piracy in the Ægean was at that time a well-organized profession, and his life was not immediately in danger; the corsairs recognized the value of their prize, a noble young Roman, head of an ancient family, attended by ten personal slaves and a private doctor. Most of Cæsar's suite were sent off to Miletus to negotiate his ransom, and he was kept on a little island in what were considered conditions of great hardship; he had only his doctor for companion, and two valets to wait on him (which shows the scale of ordinary Roman slave-households).

Although his life had been spared so far, Cæsar faced death by torture if his ransom was not forthcoming. His family was not rich for their great station in life, and he had no liquid assets nearer than Italy. He responded to this deadly danger with the fantastic, almost feverish courage which later made him the idol of his soldiers. The pirates had demanded a ransom of twenty talents (it is difficult to evaluate the currency of another age, but one talent was a lot of money, enough to keep a family in comfort). Cæsar was indignant that a Patrician Julius should be rated so low; he offered fifty talents as his true value. But he added that after he had fairly bought his life, and paid for it, he would hunt down his captors, never resting until he had seen them executed. The pirates thought this an excellent joke. While waiting for their unexpected wealth they allowed Cæsar the freedom of their island.

Cæsar carried things with a high hand. He watched the pirates practicing with their weapons, and criticized their incompetence. As a prisoner he might not join in the fencing and spear-throwing, but at wrestling and swimming he held his own. He knew that his life hung by a hair, and obviously got a thrill out of testing the patience of his captors to the limit. As a student of rhetoric he often composed themes in verse and prose; he demanded undisturbed quiet while he was at his papers, and enforced his wish; later he entertained the pirates with recitations from his own compositions, and when the ruffians seemed bored he pointed out that they were only barbarians, unfitted by their low calling to

judge Greek style. He had been regretting the neces-
sity to execute such jolly companions; but their lack of
appreciation showed that they were unworthy to cumber
the earth and he was now reconciled to their fast-
approaching end.

The pirates continued to think this bombast very
amusing. Through their agents in Miletus they learned
that Cæsar was really raising his ransom as quickly as
he could, and they made a pet of the gallant young
aristocrat who was at the same time such an excellent
investment and such an amusing companion.

Cæsar's private finances are a subject of great ob-
scurity. We know that as a young man he was deeply
in debt, and often insolvent; for his father died when he
was fourteen, he never earned money by working, and
the Cæsars were not accounted wealthy among the
ruling circles of Rome. But financiers thought him a
good risk; if he lived he would hold high office, and
every holder of high office died rich. Asia was full of
speculative financiers, and Cæsar's servants in Miletus
had no difficulty in borrowing his immense ransom.
When he had been in captivity about six weeks, the
money was paid over and he was honestly set free.

Cæsar went at once to Miletus. He had never held
any official position; but he was a Roman of Senatorial
family, a member of the small ruling class of the City
which had conquered the world. The Greek local authorities deferred to him, as a hundred years ago petty
Indian rajahs deferred to a stray European. As Rome
usually disarmed her subject-allies, Miletus had no troops

of her own, and the nearest Roman garrison was on the distant inland frontier. But there were fast merchant ships in the port, and when Cæsar called for volunteers to man them the citizens responded. He led his ships straight to the island and found that the pirates, with the feckless incompetence for which he had earlier reproached them, were still in harbor celebrating their lucky haul. Capturing all of them by surprise, he took them in chains to Pergamum, the nearest Roman headquarters. But the Roman commander was absent on campaign, and in his letters displayed too great an interest in the pirates' booty, which consisted mainly of Cæsar's borrowed fifty talents. So Cæsar ordered that the criminals should be crucified, the usual Roman penalty for felons who were not citizens. But as this was a disgustingly painful death and he owed them something for making his captivity comfortable, he had their throats cut before they were affixed to their crosses. The unrelenting punishment and the avoidance of unnecessary suffering are equally typical of Cæsar's ruthless realism. His justice was never merciful, but he never went out of his way to inflict pain for fun; and that is more than can be said of many military adventurers, or of many Romans in that last century of the Republic.

He then repaid the financiers who had advanced his ransom. The rest of the pirates' booty was distributed among the civilian volunteers who had captured it. Cæsar had levied war and condemned criminals to death without the slightest legal authority. It was an astonishing usurpation of power, but it was obviously the thing that

needed doing. Nobody complained, and many praised
him.

At the Rhodian school of rhetoric Cæsar was an outstanding pupil. But his course of study suffered frequent
interruptions. In 74 King Mithridates went to war with
Rome for his third and last try to liberate Asia from the
west. But now the old prince was desperate, seeking
any allies he could get; as he marched into the Roman
dominions he proclaimed freedom for all slaves, aboli-
tion of all debt, and free farms for everybody. The fright-
ful economic distress in some Greek cities made them
open their gates to the social revolution, but owners of
property stood by the established order. The chief Roman commander was the pro-Consul Lucius Licinius
Lucullus, but Bithynia was defended by the pro-
Consul Marcus Aurelius Cotta, Cæsar's maternal uncle.
When Mithridates, taking the Romans by surprise, advanced unopposed through Caria, Cæsar remembered
that he owed Cotta a debt for begging his life from Sulla.
He raised, on his own responsibility, another force of
unauthorized volunteers, and delayed the advance of
Mithridates until the regular Roman armies could close
the gap. This was not especially remarkable as a military
exploit, though it showed once again what many people
were beginning to realize: that young Cæsar had a way
with volunteers and was willing to take responsibility.
But politically it was a decisive action.

Sertorius still led a Popular army in Spain; Mithridates had a fleet, an advantage the military-minded Romans
seldom bothered to acquire; by sea the King was in

touch with the Popular general, and his invasion, with
its sweeping promises of better times for the poor, had
been vaguely concerted with the left-wing forces at the
other end of the Mediterranean. In fact Mithridates was
the ally of those Populars who still adhered to the program of Marius and Cinna. Cæsar, a civilian, was not
called upon to play a part. By throwing himself into the
fray he announced to the world that he was a patriotic
Roman, on the side of law and order. Henceforth he
was a respectable politician of liberal tendencies, no
longer in the eyes of old Sullan Senators a dangerous
revolutionary.

In 73 the situation in Asia was stabilized, though the
war continued. Cæsar, shortly before his twenty-seventh
birthday, disbanded his now unneeded volunteers and
returned to Rome. He found the Popular party beginning to revive, as in a free state any opposition must
revive when one party has been in control for eight years.
Servilia, the widow of Brutus, now married to Decimus
Junius Silanus, made her large town house the headquarters of the Popular organization. Cæsar naturally had
influence with a machine run by his mistress, and he was
elected Military Tribune for the year 72. This was not
a magistracy, and carried him no nearer the Senate; but
it showed that he was now respectable enough to win
votes.

In the same year began the revolt of the slaves led by
Spartacus, which for a time threatened Rome herself
with destruction. By this date the early Etruscan custom of making slaves fight one another at funerals as a

form of human sacrifice had developed into the chief
amusement of the Roman people. Public contests of
these swordsmen or gladiators were put on in special
amphitheaters, though the connection with funerals was
not forgotten and each show was dedicated to the memory of a dead man. Gladiators were of course highly
trained fencers, capable of taking on drilled troops. But
when Spartacus first seized the city of Capua there were
no trained soldiers to meet him. Sulla, as a precaution
against civil war, had stationed the whole army in the
provinces, leaving Italy unarmed; the nearest regular
forces were in Gaul or Spain, and the slave-bandits
ravaged the open country unchecked.

In 72 Sertorius was at last suppressed, and the civil
war was temporarily suspended. He was assassinated,
but Cnæus Pompeius Magnus, who had earlier defeated
his army, enjoyed the credit for restoring order in Spain.
In Asia Lucullus was getting the better of Mithridates.
He destroyed the Pontic fleet and beheaded its admiral,
a renegade Roman taken in arms against his City. This
admiral was Marcus Marius, the outlawed son of old
Caius Marius, and so first cousin to Cæsar. We are apt
to forget how disreputable were the relatives Cæsar had
to live down.

The Senate then ordered Lucullus to make peace with
Mithridates; but he led his army to the invasion of
Pontus. This was the first time a Roman general had
openly disobeyed orders from home. All the politicians of
Rome, including Cæsar, took note of the new fact that

a general at the head of a faithful army was above the law.

Spartacus was doing so well that no one was anxious to undertake the duty of destroying him. At the elections for 71 there was actually a shortage of candidates. But Pompeius was now free to return from Spain, and a new Prætor, Marcus Licinius Crassus, was given temporary command until Rome's greatest soldier could arrive. Crassus was an interesting figure, the only noble Roman who enjoyed making money as a hobby. By birth he was a Patrician and an adherent of the Optimates; his brother had been murdered by Cinna. There was a law, passed in the first instance to make corruption more difficult, which forbade Senators to engage in foreign trade; so Crassus could not do business on his own account, though he might lend money to traders. Another outlet for his business instincts, which impressed his contemporaries, was his private fire service; the trained firemen were his slaves, and they were only employed to save his property. But at that time Rome had no public fire service, and the owner of a burning house would be approached by an agent acting for Crassus; after the menaced building had been bought very cheap the firemen would save it.

A nobleman who likes money is never popular with the mob, and Crassus was despised. But he was efficient as a soldier, as he was efficient in most things. He destroyed the slave army and impressed even his pitiless contemporaries by crucifying six thousand prisoners

along the main road to the south. When Pompeius arrived from Spain he found that his work had been done
for him.

The elections for 70 were now due, and Crassus stood
for the Consulship while his glory was still fresh. It was
mildly irregular for a magistrate to stand for another office
during his year of power, for it allowed the oppressed
no interval to prosecute him as a private citizen. But
Crassus had served with distinction in the usual minor posts, and after his victory he deserved special
treatment. The Consulship might be considered his
due.

But another candidate was Pompeius, and at this
much greater irregularity the Optimates took fright. For
Pompeius, though the most famous soldier in Rome, had
never been elected to any office, and by the strict letter
of the constitution he should first serve as Quæster and
Prætor. Some Optimates talked of disallowing the illegal
candidacy, or even prosecuting Pompeius for treason; so
Pompeius, who had once been a follower of Sulla, now
sought Popular support.

He sought it from young Cæsar, who was becoming a
well-known politician of the Forum. He had not as yet
done anything praiseworthy, but he was handsome, wellborn, and an extremely good speaker. He also spent
money like water, not so much in bribes as in making
himself personally conspicuous. He was the best-dressed
man in Rome, though his clothes shocked the conservative; and not a hair on his head was ever out of place.
People liked him, as the volunteers of Miletus had liked

him; his influence was useful in getting a measure
through the Comitia.

Pompeius and Crassus were elected. Both were by
origin Optimates, but both had got in by the votes of
the Populars, and during their year of office they repaid
their supporters by repealing the changes Sulla had introduced into the constitution; they removed the disqualifi-
cation of ex-Tribunes, and arranged that judicial com-
missions should be chosen, not from the Senate, but by
ballot from the knights. Yet neither had sufficient following among the lower orders to make himself a tyrant;
those Optimates who worried about the future, in particular a rising middle-class lawyer called Marcus Tul-
lius Cicero, worried much more about the inexplicable
influence of young Cæsar, who had no public record
and yet could twist the Comitia round his finger.

Cicero was not at all a typical Roman. He was probably the greatest orator who has ever existed, and his
matchless eloquence made him prominent in that assembly of tough, commonsensical retired senior officers, the
Senate. But whereas all his colleagues quite naturally
buckled on their swords when the constitution broke
down, Cicero had no military experience, and no desire
for it. At the end of his life he faced execution with
decent courage, but he faced it from a litter, dressed in his
toga. During the civil wars he hovered ineffectually on
the sidelines, preaching reason and forbearance. His
political theories were not especially original, but he expressed them so gracefully that he was accorded more
influence than was really his due. Most Roman Senators

would have got on better in modern Burma, where
cabinets are reshuffled by the tommy-gun, than in modern Washington. Cicero is the exception, a pliant liberal
debater among the iron rulers of the Republic.

Some hotheads among the Senators considered the
possibility of framing Cæsar on a false charge of treason
before he became too powerful. But Cicero, their legal
expert, told them not to foster his campaign of self-
advertisement. He pointed out that such a fop, always
patting stray hairs into place, would never risk his neck
in the bloody game of politics. Besides, he was so polite
to the poor that he could not be ambitious. He lived
meagerly in a small house in an unfashionable quarter,
and if he went on running into debt to astonish the
voters he would soon have to flee abroad to escape his
creditors.

The Optimates won the elections for 69, and Rome
enjoyed a year of domestic peace; though Lucullus still
carried on his war in Asia, as though he were an independent ruler.

Next year Cæsar stood for the Quæstorship, the low-
est rung on the official ladder. Every year twenty Quæstors were elected as junior financial officers, and the
chief importance of the post was that it carried a seat
in the Senate. The lower age-limit, frequently infringed,
was twenty-eight; Cæsar was thirty-two.

The Quæstorship was only the first hurdle in the
obstacle race of a Roman political career. The twenty
young Quæstors chosen annually kept the Senate up to
its strength of between three and six hundred. But many

Senators never got any further, for each year from among
the ex-Quæstors were chosen ten Prætors, and from
among the ex-Prætors two Consuls. This explains the
resentment felt by ordinary Senators when a great man
blocked the avenue of promotion by repeatedly holding
the Consulship. A law laid down that two years must
elapse between two grades of office, and ten years between two Consulships; but it was so frequently disregarded that it hardly formed part of the constitution.

No one ever held the Quæstorship twice, and it must
have been hard to pick twenty young men every year
who without any public record were more worthy to be
Senators than their rivals. In fact, though the Quæstorship was an ancient office, this method of filling the
Senate was an artful dodge which Sulla had slipped into
the constitution. He could claim that the Senate em-
bodied the people's will, as every Senator had been
chosen for his post in full Comitia. Yet in fact the young
men could be chosen only as the sons of eminent fathers, or because they were backed by a political machine.
The form of election was preserved, but power lay with
the Senatorial oligarchy.

Of course Cæsar was easily elected, and in January
67, at the age of thirty-two, he took his seat in the
Senate. In the spring the Quæstors would conduct a
formal audit of the Treasury, and when the campaigning
season opened, each Prætor and Consul would nominate one of them to keep the accounts of his army.

The January session of the Senate was eventful. First
came the great pirate scare, a genuine danger which was

manipulated to give Pompeius a position of unexampled power. The Romans hated the sea, and never formed a navy of their own. In theory the contingents of those Greek subject-allies who understood the horrid business were supposed to police the Mediterranean; in practice the contingents diminished to vanishing-point, either because the Roman governor, fearing revolt, compelled the allies to disarm; or because the Greeks, who had more profitable employment for their ships, bribed the governor to say that no navy was needed in those parts. Meanwhile the stray pirates who had always infested the Mediterranean had formed a federation, with secure bases in Cilicia and Crete in which to store their booty. They had recently kidnapped two Prætors, picked up where the main road to southern Italy ran close to the coast; and Rome was hungry because corn ships from Africa and Egypt dared not leave harbor.

It was agreed that something must be done, but the Populars seized on the crisis to confer sweeping powers on their new ally Pompeius. A law was proposed in the Comitia to give him, for three years, supreme command on every sea and for fifty miles inland, with the right to demand unlimited service from the subject-allies. Normal governors would still be appointed, but they must take orders from him.

Not only was this far too much power to confer on one man, but the whole proceeding was irregular; for a law of that kind should pass the Senate before it was introduced in the Comitia. But the people complained of the high price of bread, and the commercial classes were angry at the interruption of overseas trade. Every Senator spoke against the law, with the exception of young Cæsar, faithful to the Popular cause. Then the Populars threatened civil war, and the nervous Optimates allowed the proposal to go through.

Pompeius very soon cleaned up the pirates, for he was a good soldier. But any competent pro-Consul could have done as much; the extraordinary powers had been needed only to gratify his ambition and his vanity.

Meanwhile Cæsar was making himself even better-known than before, by a series of actions which surprised conventional Romans. When his aunt Julia died, Cæsar, as head of the family, gave her the splendid public funeral that was her birthright. In the long procession walked actors impersonating magistrates of the Julian house for the last four hundred years; but what excited the crowd, in particular the watching Populars, was that the lady's husband, seven times Consul and the greatest Roman of his day, was represented with all his marks of dignity; though the Senate, at the instigation of Sulla, had declared the memory of Marius infamous. Every Popular could now take pride in the memory of the famous soldier, with the added joy of seeing the government swallow a breach of the law which it feared to punish.

In the Forum the body was laid on a great pyre of wood, and the head of the family spoke a conventional eulogy before the torch was applied. Cæsar's speech contained little about his aunt, for Roman ladies were supposed to live unnoticed (it was high praise to say

of a wife that she was unknown even to her neighbors).
Instead he reminded his hearers of the nobility of the
Julian house, descended from Ancus Martius, king of
Rome, and from the goddess Venus. "Our stock has
therefore both the sanctity of kings and the claim to
reverence of gods, who are greater than kings." It was a
high claim, coming from a citizen speaking to fellow
citizens.

Soon afterward Cæsar lost his much-loved wife, Cornelia, mother of his only child, Julia. He gave her also a
public funeral, with a speech in the Forum. He was
within his rights, for she had been wife to the head of a
great family. But heretofore only elderly matrons had
been eulogized in public, and it was unprecedented to
pay such honor to a lady dead in the prime of life (Cornelia was in her early thirties). Cæsar was reiterating in
public a point he often made in private conversation,
that there was something special about his family, descended from gods and kings; it was right to grant to a
Julia honors denied to the common herd.

The Populars enjoyed it all. The mob admires im-
pudence, and it was fun to remind stuffy old Senators
that some of the very best blood in Rome was on the
other side.

Cæsar was nominated to the staff of the pro-Prætor
in the Bætic province of Spain, and in that summer saw
for the first time the barbarian west, where he would
make his name. But in political circles he was already
well known, and now the anecdotes cluster thickly. It is
said that as he rode past the western end of the Alps

(Romans never voyaged by sea if the journey could be made by land) he noted a squalid little barbarian village. Turning to his companion, he confessed that he would rather be first in that little hole than second in Rome, for he could not endure to be second anywhere. In Spain he saw a statue of Alexander the Great, exposed for veneration in a temple. At the sight he was overcome by sorrow, and explained that it was because Alexander had conquered the known world by the age of thirty-three, and what had Cæsar, who was older, done with his life so far?

He returned from Spain before his appointment was finished, which was technically illegal; but his contemporaries were tremendously impressed to see a politician forgo some weeks of office. He got back in time to stand for election as Ædile. Ædiles were not important functionaries, though the two Patricians among them were honored with ivory thrones and other marks of dignity. But though the office brought no power, it offered enormous opportunities for self-advertisement, for the Ædiles presented the shows which were part of the state religion; it had become the custom for them to pay for these Games out of their own pockets, and an Ædile who displayed unusual generosity would be remembered by the populace when he sought election to more important office.

That autumn there was great political activity in Rome. Pompeius had suppressed the pirates, largely by granting free pardons to all who laid down their arms (so that piracy broke out again as soon as his back was turned); but in roving through Asia he had inevitably collided with Lucullus. Lucullus had been abroad for so long that no one was certain which party he supported; but there was no doubt that Pompeius was now a leader of the Populars, and their excellent organization backed him in the Comitia. Before his special commission had expired he was given three more years of supreme power in the east, with the task of liquidating Mithridates once and for all.

Pompeius was a very good soldier. He was so obviously the right man for this difficult job that his appointment was favored by all parties; Cicero spoke for the moderate Optimates, and Cæsar for the Populars, until for once the Senate agreed with the Comitia. The only dissenting voice came from Lucullus, who tried to imitate Sulla in leading a Roman army after his formal deposition from command; but his men refused to follow him, and he returned to peaceful retirement in Italy. Long campaigning in the east had gained him enormous wealth and accustomed him to un-Roman forms of luxury; he introduced new fruits and flowers to Italy, and applied himself to debauchery in the traditional manner of the retired Roman general.

That autumn Cæsar married a lady named Pompeia, who was not related to Cnæus Pompeius Maximus (as he was now called), the most eminent living Roman. Her father had been Quintus Pompeius Rufus, Sulla's colleague in the Consulship, murdered in 88; her mother was Cornelia, daughter of the great Dictator. The nephew of Marius had espoused the granddaughter of

Sulla; which might prove that at last the wounds of civil war were healed, or merely that eminent politicians of all parties were coming closer together, in mutual contempt for the common herd.

In the year 65, when Cæsar was Curule Ædile, parties were fluid. Only the mob now cared about the domestic affairs of Rome, and no great constitutional issues were pending. The prize for which great men contended was the Consulship. By this time the Consuls in office performed only the boring tasks of presiding over the Comitia and offering the state sacrifices; but for the following year at least, often for two or three years, an ex-Consul was invariably given a pro-Consular province, with command of a great army. That was the summit of Roman ambition. A pro-Consul might win a war, to be granted the supreme honor of a Triumph, an honor which would be recalled at every funeral in his family until the end of time. Even if he was honest he would certainly amass an enormous fortune in presents from successful litigants. If he won the affection of his men he might lead his army against Rome and rule there as both Marius and Sulla had ruled in the past. As the personalities of the holders of these great offices hardly affected the common voter, there was scope for combinations and shiftings of allegiance.

Cæsar, during his Ædileship, took a hand in this great game. His first object was to increase his personal influence with the mob, for control of the mob was his only asset; he had never commanded regular troops, and in the eyes of famous generals like Pompeius and Crassus he was a civilian manager, useful at public meetings, but of course quite insignificant if ever it should come to drawn swords.

Cæsar's colleague as Patrician, or Curule, Ædile was Marcus Calpurnius Bibulus, not a clever man but the author of one very witty remark. For he said that he was considering changing his name to Pollux. One of the most famous temples in Rome was that dedicated to the Twin Brethren, Castor and Pollux; but in ordinary conversation it was always called the temple of Castor. In the same way the expense of the public Games was shared by the two Curule Ædiles, but no one called them anything except the magnificent Games given by Cæsar. They were the most splendid in the history of the City. On one day Cæsar exhibited 320 pairs of gladiators, all wearing silver armor; for another show he assembled so many slave-swordsmen that the Senate, fearing that they might break loose and sack the City, compelled him to disperse them before the fight.

Cæsar was notoriously in financial difficulties, but there was no secret about the source of his funds. He had made an alliance with Crassus, the richest man in Rome; which meant of course that he must repay Crassus by using his influence in the Comitia. Crassus, the con-queror of Spartacus, was eager for more military glory; he sought a commission to annex Egypt, a nominally independent kingdom whose successive governments were then as weak and transient as they are now. That would give him a great army, and enable him to talk to Pompeius on equal terms. But Pompeius still enjoyed

the esteem of both parties, and the scheme never got
through the Senate.

With help from Crassus drying up, Cæsar was in
desperate straits for money. As a last resort he gave his
sister Julia in marriage to Caius Octavius, a vulgar moneylender and, what was even lower in Roman eyes, a
country bumpkin who lived in the little town of Vel-
letri. But all would come right in the end, if only his
creditors would be patient. He had expended a vast sum
on a very famous and expensive Ædileship; if he could
keep his head above water for a year or two, he must
get in return the governorship of a rich province.

Meanwhile the small knot of leading politicians was
knitting closer together. Pompeius and Crassus had begun as Optimates, while Cæsar had been born a Popular; but they were united in despising the flighty and
corrupt electorate. They were constantly in and out of
each other's houses, and smart society was amused to
note that while Pompeius was absent in the east Cæsar
became the lover of his wife, Mucia.

In the next year Cæsar was appointed to preside over
the special court which investigated assassinations. Of
his two rivals, Crassus was still angling for the Egyptian
command, and Pompeius was conquering Syria. Nothing could demonstrate more clearly Cæsar's status as a
party-boss and manager of the Comitia; while others led
great armies, his job was to arrange convictions and ac-
quittals with one eye on the next elections. As a matter
of fact the elections for 63 gave a great deal of trouble.
There were seven candidates for the Consulship. One

was Cicero, the best speaker of his age and in many ways
a thoroughly suitable man, but a leader of the Optimates;
others were Caius Antonius Hybrida, whom Cæsar had
prosecuted unsuccessfully in 77, and Lucius Sergius Catalina, a rash adventurer who was an embarrassment to
both parties. For he had undoubtedly arranged the murder of Populars at the behest of Sulla, the very crime
the assassination court had been set up to punish; but he
was now under the protection of Crassus and was running, against the regular machine, as an extreme Popular.
The Optimates hastened to prosecute him for murders
committed sixteen years earlier, murders which at the
time they had thoroughly approved; and Cæsar, who
was supposed to be the avenger of the innocent blood
shed by Sulla, was ordered by Crassus, his paymaster, to
see that the prosecution came to nothing. Cæsar managed
this by adjourning the case until the election was over
and no one cared what happened to Catalina. But his
reputation suffered, and he could no longer pose as the
disinterested righter of wrongs done to the followers of
Marius.

The candidates elected were Cicero, an orator who
could win any election on any program so long as he
might address the voters undisturbed; and Hybrida, a
lesser light of the Optimate party. For the time being,
the Populars had lost control of the Comitia.

In 63, the year of Cicero's eventful Consulship,
Cæsar made more than one effort to return to the center
of the stage. He proposed to reinstate the children of

those Populars who had been killed by Sulla, and whose family estates had of course been confiscated.

But Cicero, who genuinely feared a social revolution, argued that this was not the moment to make far-reaching changes in the ownership of property (for of course these estates had been freely bought and sold for the last twenty-seven years); and the greatest orator in Rome, with the added prestige of the Consulship, persuaded the Comitia to turn down the proposal.

Cæsar's second effort took the form of an elaborate joke, worth relating to demonstrate Roman reverence for the letter of the ancient laws. Caius Rabirius was an elderly and insignificant Senator of the Optimate faction, who occasionally boasted of the one great deed which had been the highlight of his dim career; nearly forty years before, in the year 100, he had made one of the mob who broke into prison to lynch the Popular leaders, and he claimed to be the actual slayer of Saturninus.

Cæsar suddenly took notice of this ancient crime; but instead of charging Rabirius before his own assassination court, he impeached him by an archaic procedure for the crime of sacrilege in laying hands on the sacred person of a Tribune. The case fell to be judged by two magistrates chosen by lot, and as the official dice were known to be loaded, no one was surprised when the lot indicated Cæsar himself and his kinsman Lucius Cæsar. Rabirius was found guilty on his own confession, and received the only sentence permitted by the ancient law. His sacrilege rendered him so unclean that even the executioner might

not touch him; he must be suspended from an unlucky
and barren fruit tree until he perished of exposure.

Of course no one really wanted to kill the old man,
especially as by this time exile had replaced death as
the normal punishment for Roman citizens convicted of
serious crime. But the sentence stood until a competent
authority should intervene. Luckily a Consul had power
to quash it, which was what Cicero did immediately.
But he then got the Senate to pass a resolution deploring
any further persecution of Rabirius, and that annoyed
the Populars, as an invasion of the rights of the Comitia.
A Tribune indicted Rabirius before the Council of the
Plebs. Then the Urban Prætor, a legal expert, transferred
the case to the Comitia (where Patricians, debarred from
attending the Council of the Plebs, might speak and
vote). Cicero, speaking for the defense, made another
tactical mistake. He said that any violent deed done by
Rabirius was covered by the Senate's Ultimate Decree.
But this was the great constitutional battleground of
Populars and Optimates, and the Populars would kill
the old man rather than yield the point of principal.
Things looked very black for Rabirius; but before the
Comitia came to voting, it was dispersed in an unusual
fashion. A Prætor lowered the red flag which normally
flew from the fortress of Janiculum just across the Tiber,
and the strict letter of the constitution enacted that after
noting this signal of alarm all citizens should fall in,
armed, to repel the threatened Etruscan invasion. The
Etruscans had been conquered long before, and it was
as though nowadays the United States Senate should

adjourn an awkward debate on the excuse that Confederate troops were marching on Washington. But everyone was delighted to find such an amusing and legal way out of the impasse, and Rabirius was never troubled again.

This little joke displayed Cæsar's antiquarian knowledge and mastery of legal procedure, both qualities highly esteemed in Rome. To us it seems odd, but it increased his reputation.

About this time fell vacant the life-appointment of *Pontifex Maximus*, or High Priest of Rome; and it is typical of the Roman habit of bringing religion into ordinary politics that the next Pontifex was to be appointed by a vote of the Comitia. The daily life of the Pontifex Maximus was hedged by numerous tabus (for example, he might never see a dead body, and if he had no wife an official substitute shared his table, though not his bed). The office, which carried great prestige and many perquisites but no political power, was traditionally reserved for elder statesmen whom a life of service to the community had condemned to a poverty-stricken old age. But Cæsar, who had never commanded an army or held any office greater than Ædile, announced his candidature. The election was hotly contested, and as no political principles were involved, the only method of persuasion was bribery. Cæsar spent so much borrowed money that when he went down to the Forum on election day he told his mother that he must return as Pontifex Maximus or not at all; if he was beaten he must flee the City to avoid his creditors.

However, he was elected, and for the rest of his life

enjoyed the prestige and precedence of the High Priest of Rome. He moved from his little apartment in the unfashionable Suburra to a handsome official residence, and wore on public occasions the splendid robes of his post. As for the ceremonial tabus, he declared, in his official capacity as interpreter of the will of the gods, that they bound the Pontifex only while he lived in Rome; when he had crossed the sacred Pomœrium they no longer affected him.

The elections for next year passed off peacefully, though both the Consuls chosen were Optimates. Cæsar himself was elected Prætor, the next step on the official ladder which he was climbing so slowly and unremarkably. So that by the autumn he enjoyed both the great personal sanctity of the Pontifex Maximus and the precedence in the Senate of a Prætor-elect.

It was just as well, for that winter he needed all his assets. When Cicero in the last weeks of his Consulship denounced the still mysterious conspiracy of Catilina, many Senators suspected that Cæsar was mixed up in it. What Catilina was after is disputed to this day; but he seems to have hoped to cancel all debt, or at least his own debts; and he may have planned to seize the City by a sudden rising of armed conspirators. He had just lost his second campaign for the Consulship, and he would rather fight than go bankrupt. Cicero handled him with cautious but successful strategy. There was no evidence against him that would stand up in court, but the matchless invective of the Consul drove him in the end to flee the City and join an insignificant band of desperate revolutionaries; rather than surrender, he died sword in hand. In the meanwhile Cicero had carried in the Senate the Ultimate Decree, and by its authority proposed to kill various citizens suspected of complicity in the revolt.

Like any community that rests on slavery, Rome was always deeply afraid of a revolution from below. Not only the Optimates were hot against Catilina; the middle classes, normally Popular, feared for their property. It seemed that Cicero would easily persuade the Senate to sanction the proposed executions.

But Cæsar stood by his principles. He was a Popular, bound by his political creed to deny the force of the Ultimate Decree; he also disapproved of using the death sentence as a convenient way to close the career of a suspected revolutionary against whom there was no evidence. He advocated the punishment of exile instead, and he spoke so well that he nearly persuaded the Senate to vote down Cicero, the great orator. But Marcus Porcius Cato, a gloomy statesman who in his heart favored the execution of most of the human race, spoke for immediate death; and the Senate, in a sudden revulsion of feeling, turned on Cæsar. When the suspects were promptly killed, he nearly shared their fate. Optimates spoke against him in such threatening tones that he thought it wise to leave the Senate House, and as he passed a group of armed knights who had volunteered to guard Cicero during the crisis they menaced him with drawn swords. For the first and last time in his life Cæsar was genuinely afraid. He did not again appear in public until the conspiracy of Catilina had been wound up.

There is no reason to suppose that Cæsar had conspired, save that he was one of the spendthrift nobles who would gain by a cancelation of debt (which would not profit the really poor). But he and Catilina enjoyed the same kind of wild party, and they had often met socially. A year earlier Cæsar had fixed a political prosecution for him; but that was probably because Crassus had ordered it, not because he felt any sympathy for Optimates who had committed murder in the interests of Sulla. But to the average Roman the conspiracy seemed a very shocking affair, just the kind of thing that would happen in times when penniless Ædiles exhibited 320 pairs of gladiators in silver armor and stood for election to the High Priesthood before they were forty years old. Public opinion underwent a strong conservative reaction, and Cæsar's influence diminished.

Therefore in 62, his year of office as Prætor, he strengthened himself by obsequious service to Pompeius. That great general was in the last year of his eastern command; he had committed himself to a mass of territorial and financial settlements which must presently be ratified by the Senate; and he would like to be offered another extraordinary command in the near future, though he considered it beneath his dignity to ask for it. In all these things Cæsar could be very useful to him.

But in domestic politics Pompeius was remarkably maladroit. He could never lower himself to persuade, yet he was too honorable to use threats. Cæsar, to earn his gratitude, proposed a law that would transfer to the great man a most valuable job, the rebuilding of the temple of Jupiter on the Capitol. The overseeing of this work carried with it considerable patronage, valuable perquisites, and a position of great dignity; but it had long been promised, as under an oligarchy such things are promised in advance, to Quintus Lutatius Catulus, a noble ex-Consul whose high repute did not rest on the foundation of any concrete achievement. The Senate refused the proposal, and Cæsar was publicly snubbed.

During the winter his private life became the talk of Rome. The episode is not important politically, but it is very famous, and must be mentioned. The annual mysteries of the Good Goddess, which only women might see, were held at the official residence of the Pontifex Maximus under the presidency of his wife. A noble young rake named Publius Clodius (whose eloquence had persuaded the troops of Lucullus to submit to Pompeius) attended the meeting disguised as a woman. It was said that he was pursuing an intrigue with Pompeia, but he may have gone only to satisfy his curiosity. He was recognized, and the resulting scandal was all the more exciting because the Senatorial commission of inquiry thought that at last they might discover what their wives did at this festival.

Cæsar immediately divorced Pompeia, sending her back to her kin without explanation or excuse, as was the right of any Roman husband. But to the Senatorial commission he protested that he had no evidence to give, for on the famous evening he had been absent from

his house, as every man should be on the night of this
mystery. A Senator asked him why, in that case, he had
divorced his wife; and he made the celebrated reply
that the wife of Cæsar must be above suspicion. The
emphasis was on *Cæsar*, implying that the Julian house
was greater and more sacred than others. It was in line
with the eulogy at his aunt's funeral, a claim to be in
some undefined way more important than his fellow citizens.

In 61 Cæsar set out to govern Further Spain, the
province allotted to him for the usual two years' tenure
of command that was the normal reward of the Prætorship. He could not leave Rome until he had borrowed
the enormous sum of 850 talents from Crassus to keep
his creditors quiet until his return. For the first time in
his life, at the age of thirty-nine, he commanded regular
troops; but there was no more than the usual unrest
among the Spanish mountaineers, and his police operations could hardly be called campaigning. He mitigated
a local financial crisis, and was in general liked by his
subjects. But his administration was no better than would
be expected from any competent pro-Prætor, and in
Rome it made no particular stir. Once again, as when
he had been Quæstor in the same country, he cut short
his term of office to reach Rome in time for the elections.

It was a period of political tension. Pompeius had
entered Rome in the splendid Triumph which celebrated
his conquest of Mithridates; but he had discharged his
soldiers before the Senate had ratified the treaties he had
concluded, and the Senators, moved by a natural jeal-

ousy, kept on adjourning the ratifications, including the most important point of all, the veterans' bonus which Pompeius had promised to his men. He should have kept his army in being, as a threat to the Senate; but if he now recalled it, that would be open rebellion. The great man was not really at home as a leader of the Populars, for their program shocked his conservative instincts. Yet the Optimates were amusing themselves by making him look foolish. He grumbled at every dinner-table, a hero at the mercy of petty intriguers. If only some politician who knew the ropes would arrange to get him, legally, the command of another army!

Rome's second soldier, Crassus, was also at odds with the Senate. He was still making money in large quantities and lending it lavishly to finance the campaign of any promising statesman, but no one remembered him as the conqueror of Spartacus, or agreed with his own estimate of his military capacity. He felt that he had it in him to win a great war and enjoy a resounding Triumph; but the world saw him as an unscrupulous speculator, and the Senate would not offer him one of the great military commands.

Cæsar, viewing things in perspective from his distant Spanish standpoint, recognized an opening for a clever leader of the Comitia. Pompeius and Crassus were personally on bad terms, for retired generals are usually jealous of one another. But neither would be jealous of Cæsar, the civilian party-boss who had never fought a war. If he could bring them together, their combined influence would make certain his own election to the Consulship, and as Consul he could see that they were given commands worthy of their talents. It was a fairly obvious measure of mutual self-help, but only Cæsar's charm in private intercourse and his skill in swaying the Comitia could reconcile conflicting interests to bring it to fruition.

His first plan had been for a grand coalition, to include Cicero, the hero of the middle classes, and Cato, the leader of the ultra-conservatives. But neither Cicero nor Cato would join. Both thought of themselves as servants of the Senate, and refused personal power for themselves as a reward for suppressing their fellow Senators.

Perhaps it is wrong to describe Cato as the leader of the conservatives. Often he had no followers at all, though the Senate always listened respectfully to his views. He was an eccentric who had hit on an original remedy for the disorders of the times: two hundred years ago Rome had been happy and united; let the Romans behave in every detail of their lives as though it *was* two hundred years ago, and the strife of parties would vanish.

He carried out this program in his own person. The Ancestors had gone barefoot; so Cato never wore shoes, even when presiding over important lawsuits. The Ancestors wore no hats; so he marched bareheaded under the sun of Africa. The Ancestors had certain less pleasant characteristics, and Cato followed them unflinchingly. If parsimony, cruelty to slaves, and a general puritanical hatred of enjoyment were ancestral traits, Cato would be meaner, a harder slave-driver, a more grudging killjoy, than any other Roman citizen. He really loved Liberty, as he proved later; but he had the greatest contempt for the Pursuit of Happiness, and he abandoned Life when it was no longer worth living.

So when Cæsar announced his candidature for the Consular election for the year 59, he was not the leader of a coalition of all parties, but the candidate of the Populars, opposed by the full organization of the Optimates. This opposition at once made itself felt. It was against the spirit of the ancient constitution for a pro-Prætor to stand for election while holding office, though in recent years exceptions had been freely granted; when Cæsar applied for an exception, the Senate refused it. The Optimates hoped that he would not sacrifice half a year of command to be Consul next winter, when it was obvious that such an orator must be Consul before he died. But Cæsar at once relinquished his command and came back to Italy.

The Senate then devised another obstacle. Cæsar's suppression of a rebellion in western Spain might entitle him to a Triumph, the highest honor Rome could bestow on a citizen. But a Triumph, which marked the return of a victorious general, might be enjoyed only at his entry into Rome. The Optimates let it be known that Cæsar would be granted a Triumph after election day.

An average Roman would sacrifice anything for a Triumph. But Cæsar (who had no legitimate son) was unconventionally disdainful of hereditary honors. He dismissed his ceremonial bodyguard, slipped into Rome as a private citizen, and was elected Consul.

It is a sign of the weakness of Roman party ties that so often the two Consuls were chosen from opposing parties. As each century voted for two Consuls, this would only be the outcome of cross-voting, based proba-bly on feelings of kinship or locality. Cæsar's colleague in the Consulship of 59 was Bibulus, the Optimate who six years before had complained of his overshadowing profusion as Ædile.

It was the duty of the Senate to fix in advance the provinces which the Consuls would govern after their year of office. To annoy Cæsar the Senators announced that the Consular provinces for 58 would be Forests and Rights of Way, the dimmest field of administration at their disposal. Cæsar's faithful Populars countered by passing a law which took the assignment of provinces from the Senate and gave it to the Comitia.

The Consulship of 59 is usually taken as marking the beginning of the *Triumvirate*, or Rule of Three Men; though that is hindsight and contemporaries did not no-tice it immediately. But next year, when Cæsar had his pro-Consular command and had given commands to Pompeius and Crassus, those three would in fact rule Rome. Of course they could keep power only so long as they worked with one another, and family alliances were arranged to keep them friendly. Cæsar himself mar-ried Calpurnia, whose father, Calpurnius Piso, a left-wing Popular, was promised the Consulship in 58 as dowry. Pompeius married Cæsar's only child, Julia, whose father had been the acknowledged lover of her predecessor. The Triumvirate was an unsavory business, and the best speakers in Rome, who were the Optimate leaders, made some savage and true observations.

Cato, protesting at the arrangement in favor of Piso, said that it was shameful to see Roman armies bartered in marriage settlements. He characterized Crassus as "a usurer whose vote in the Senate was for sale, and who could be hired to make scoundrels respectable by inviting them to his official receptions." Pompeius was "the comic hero of a war without battles, who had married the daughter of his first wife's lover." Cæsar was hardly important enough to merit abuse; all that was known of him was that he had been the accomplice of Catilina and the boy-friend of King Nicomedes.

Cæsar, replying as Consul to the debate, reveled in the scandals of his past. With Nicomedes he had played a feminine part, but what of that? Queen Semiramis had done great deeds.

Cæsar's whole term of office was stormy. His first task was to reward the veterans of Pompeius; but in this he was strongly opposed by the other Consul, Bibulus. His law was eventually passed after a good-tempered riot, whose organization displayed the well-known sense of humor of Clodius. Bibulus was attacked in the Comitia, but not harmed. He was merely crowned with an inverted dustbin, to the detriment of his robes of office; while the ceremonial rods of his Lictors were broken over their heads.

After this, Bibulus dared not oppose the Populars in

Comitia. He remained at home, and tried to paralyze
the legislature by announcing each morning omens so
unfavorable that no public business should be transacted.
This was part of the duty of a Consul, for the state religion was much concerned with omens. But the Populars were by tradition scoffers at Patrician priestly rites,
and Bibulus overplayed his hand by making these an-
nouncements too often. As it was evident that he did not
himself believe what he said, the Comitia disregarded
him.

Yet his efforts were not without effect. Cæsar and
Clodius in conjunction could pass any law, and when
passed it must be obeyed. But by passing laws on unlucky days Cæsar was breaking the letter of the constitution, and another administration might not only cancel
all his acts, but prosecute him as well. While he held
office no one could touch him, but as a private citizen
he would be in danger.

The Triumvirs, though they controlled the Comitia,
could not compete in the Senate with the eloquence of
Cicero, or with Cato's appeal to ancestral prejudice.
They themselves were of course Senators, who must
attend regularly, and they grew very tired of these un-
answerable attacks. Arrangements were made to buy
their chief accusers, or to silence them by other means.
Cato was offered a lucrative piece of graft, the formal
annexation of Cyprus and the assessment of its taxes,
which should mean bribes from every wealthy Cypriot.
He was so old-fashioned that he missed the point, but
he thought it his duty to serve the state whenever asked.

He went off to Cyprus, where he refused all bribes and drew up an honest assessment. That got him out of the way with no hard feelings.

Cicero was a harder nut to crack. He refused several good offers, though his brother accepted a well-rewarded appointment on Cæsar's staff. The only way to silence him was to frighten him, and this was easy, for he had a skeleton in his cupboard. His execution of the accomplices of Catilina was in Popular eyes illegal.

But only one man could win a prosecution against Cicero's defense, and that man could not stand for the Tribunate which would make him the prosecutor. Clodius had now organized a gang who could carry any law through the Comitia by the simple process of beating up the opposition; but he was by birth a Patrician of the great Claudian house (he deliberately misspelled his name to make it look less aristocratic), and no Patrician could be Tribune. He sought adoption into a Plebeian family. But such an important change of status, though recognized by the law, needed the ratification of the Pontifex Maximus, and Cæsar hesitated. He admired Cicero, and hoped to win his friendship; if only the orator would accept a bribe, Clodius would remain muzzled.

Cicero was obstinate, and Cæsar sanctioned the adoption. As soon as Clodius was Tribune he brought in a bill to punish past illegalities, obviously aimed at Cicero personally. Cicero went to Greece to avoid prosecution, and the Triumvirs were no longer made to look foolish in the Senate.

At the end of the year Cæsar received the pro-
Consular command that was his due; but as a politician
and leader in the Comitia he ought to stay as near to
Rome as possible. He was granted a special command,
for five years, in the provinces of Illyria (at the head of
the Adriatic) and Cisalpine Gaul (which is now Italy
between the Po and the Alps); as there were no troops
in Italy proper, that gave him the army nearest to the
City, and he was only a few days' ride from the center
of politics. Both provinces were peaceful; which was
just as well, as their new governor had little military experience.

Then Metellus, governor of Transalpine Gaul (the
Mediterranean coast of France), died suddenly; and the
vacant province was offered to Cæsar, as an afterthought
and because no one else wanted it.

In March 58, in his forty-second year, Cæsar set off
for his provinces.

It was nine years before he saw the City again, and
during those nine years of his forties Cæsar proved himself a great general. It was an astonishing transformation.
He had entered late on his public career, delaying to
avoid the enmity of Sulla; and many of his contemporaries had already commanded armies. It is important to
bear in mind, during all the negotiations which followed,
that Roman opinion regarded him primarily as a politician of the Comitia to whom speechmaking came more
easily than fighting. But next time he saw the Forum it
was as the leader of a victorious rebel army.

CHAPTER FIVE

CÆSAR IN GAUL

OF CÆSAR's three provinces, Illyria hardly concerns us. The mountains at the head of the Adriatic were sparsely inhabited by poor and fierce barbarians, whose natural in-clination to piracy was hampered only by the dearth of merchant ships to plunder. Cæsar usually went there once a year to preside in the law court, but otherwise Illyria did not bother him. Cisalpine Gaul was different. When Rome was founded, Gallic tribes held all Italy north of the Appennines; it was these Gauls who had once sacked Rome; from them came the famous horde who marched down the Danube, plundered Thessaly and Thrace, were barely turned from Delphi, and ended in Asia as the Galatians. They had been mighty warriors, fair-haired giants, more than a match for Romans in hand-to-hand conflict. Now Rome had conquered them, chiefly because they would never unite behind their kings; but historically minded Romans still shuddered when they heard of a Gallic "tumult" on the Po.

Yet these southern Gauls were rapidly turning into Italians. Every year more of them lived in cities and spoke Latin at the fireside; there was less and less dif-ference between them and the genuine Romans (who had no color-bar or contempt for foreigners). Some of them had acquired Roman citizenship as individuals, and there was a feeling, especially among the Populars, that it was time to extend Italian privileges to all the land south of the Alps. The country was also in process of settlement by discharged Roman veterans, whose bonus farms clustered round new towns. If politics had not intervened—the Optimates did not want to diminish the number of first-class pro-Consular provinces—Cisalpine Gaul would have become part of Italy in the time of Sulla.

Transalpine Gaul, which is now southern France, was also a peaceful land. Marseilles was an ancient and civilized Greek city, and the district near it, still called Provence, had taken rapidly to Roman ways. It was not wealthy, just a rocky coast with a savage hinterland and a trickle of trade up the Rhone valley to the unknown barbarous north. But strategically it was most important, as the road to the silver mines of Spain. Because the northern frontier was undefined, it needed, and was given, the considerable garrison of four legions.

Henceforth we have Cæsar's own books as a record of his actions, and though *The Gallic War* is a work of propaganda, written with the superb art which conceals art, it does not tell downright lies. Even more important than the record of events, it gives us an insight into Cæsar's mind; read carefully, it shows us what he thought of barbarians.

He was a keen student of the barbarian world, though what interests modern anthropologists did not always interest him. He never picked up any of the local languages, and as he relied on interpreters he seldom noticed whether a particular tribe spoke Celtic or German. In his

tidy mind Germans lived east of the Rhine, and everybody west of it must be a Gaul; though he noted that
the Belgians, west of the river, behaved very like Germans. What he wanted to know, and what he learned
very thoroughly, was the geography of the land, with
the strength of its fortresses and the exact line of tribal
boundaries. He also inquired very carefully into the number of fighting-men in each tribe, and above all into its
manner of government. The Gauls at this period were
moving away from hereditary monarchy to government
by a vague council of nobles, which Cæsar calls a republic; but monarchy was still remembered, and every
leader hoped to make himself a king. Each tribe was
riddled with personal animosities, and rivals of a popular
chief were always willing to call in the national enemy.

The Gauls were often on the move, and it was a
threat from a people by the headwaters of the Rhine
which had brought Cæsar hurrying from Rome. The
Helvetii wished to migrate to Aquitaine, which was not
Roman territory; but they wished to traverse a narrow
belt of the Roman province to get there. The Roman
commanders on the spot were willing to permit this,
chiefly because they considered that their available force
could not prevent it; but when Cæsar arrived, he first
temporized to allow reinforcements to come up, and
then announced that any invasion would be repelled by
arms at the very frontier.

In his whole command there were four veteran legions, and he had been recruiting two others in Italy;
but at Geneva he had only one legion and some recruits

from another. With this force, which cannot have ex-
ceeded 5,000 men, he built an entrenchment eighteen
miles long and held it against a halfhearted barbarian
attack.

For the most wonderful thing about Cæsar, the thing
that has made him famous to the present day, was his
skill in handling Roman troops. It is time to explain the
organization of the Roman army. The basic unit was the
legion of heavy infantry, nominally 6,000 strong; but
after deducting sick and casualties a legion could seldom
put more than 4,000 men in line; we shall see that two
weak legions which Cæsar took to Alexandria, after
fierce fighting in the Civil War, together made up only
3,000 men. The legion was divided into ten cohorts,
each about the size of a weak battalion, and the cohort
into six centuries, normally containing fewer than 100
men. These men were all swordsmen, trained to fight
individually with the large square Roman shield and the
short Spanish broadsword; besides their shields they wore
metal helmets, and metal scales on their leather jerkins;
but they were on the whole less heavily defended than
the Greek hoplites whom they overcame in the east. The
greatest difference between a Greek and a Roman soldier
was that the legionary carried no spear; he had instead
two javelins, which he threw at the last moment before
the hostile lines collided; then he went in with sword
and shield. Romans fought in very open order. The
normal battle formation was three lines each of three
ranks, every man at arm's length from his neighbor. So
a Roman force held a very much longer front than the

same number of Greeks, packed shoulder to shoulder in sixteen ranks behind their long Macedonian pikes, or than an equal number of barbarians crowding together to keep up their courage.

Since the days of Marius the Roman army had become completely professional. The draft remained on the statute book to fill the ranks in an emergency, but in practice every man was a volunteer, enlisted for twenty years' service. As in the armies of eighteenth-century Europe, he bought his food and equipment from his pay; that left him only a little pocket money, but he had a good chance of growing rich from plunder, including the sale as slaves of prisoners captured in war; and he looked to his commander to get him a farm or its equivalent in cash when he came to retire. For the bond between commander and soldier was very close; the oath of allegiance, annually renewed, said nothing about serving the City of Rome; it was a promise to obey the commander, by name. That was one reason why ambitious generals could usually count on their men to follow them, even into rebellion.

The Roman army was by far the best-disciplined force of its day. Occasionally a whole unit would mutiny, or refuse duty in the manner of modern strikers. But, apart from these exceptional circumstances, when a legion was ordered to march twenty miles, then build a fortified camp and post sentries before settling down for the night (which were the orders for most legions on every day of the campaigning season), the commander could count on obedience; the legion would be in the right place next morning, with no stragglers; and the country, if friendly, would not have been pillaged. Not every modern general can rely on such certain obedience.

This very high standard of discipline meant that the Roman army could manage with very few officers. In fact, by our notions they had no regimental officers at all. Each century was led by a centurion, promoted from the ranks; the 60 centurions of the legion were ranged in a hierarchy, led by the first centurion of the first century of the first cohort, and promotion was by seniority from the sixtieth century to the first. In addition the bearer of the regimental Eagle, a sacred standard treated with all the reverence due to an emblem of the skygod, was a respected warrant-officer, chosen for his steadiness in the field; and the bearers of the lesser standards of the cohorts held a certain authority. But the only commissioned officers in the whole legion, a force equivalent to a modern division, were the legate in command, who was the personally chosen deputy of the commander in chief, and a few Military Tribunes. The army was run by generals, colonels, and sergeants.

So far we have spoken only of infantry of the line. That is because the regular Roman army contained no other troops. The knights who had once made up the regular cavalry were now merely an upper grade of citizens with a property-qualification; though young knights who hoped to be Senators sometimes served on the commander's staff, as Cæsar had served on the staff of Minutius Thermus. The contingents of the subject-allies supplied the other arms. Cæsar in Gaul had detachments of slingers and archers from Africa and the Balearics. But in the west there were no allies who could contribute cavalry; as horse Cæsar had to hire local barbarian mercenaries.

On the battlefield the legion might be nothing but infantry of the line, but its ranks contained an astonishing number of craftsmen. The Tenth Legion, Cæsar's favorite corps, could furnish a mounted escort if horses were provided. Every man in the ranks could use a spade, and in fact did so every evening; for after the march the army always dug itself in for the night behind a high earthen rampart crowned with sharp wooden stakes. There was no separate corps of engineers because the whole army could undertake advanced engineering work; at a moment's notice a legion could construct a bridge over a deep river, beginning by felling suitable trees in the forest; and in the leisure of winter-quarters detachments of troops chosen at random could build ocean-going transports, first forging the nails which would hold them together. In an emergency a chance-gathered fatigue party could make one serviceable ship out of two damaged ones. Every Roman general depended on long lines of strong entrenchments, as much as he depended on the broadswords of his men; and he took it for granted that when he marched through trackless country he would leave a first-class road behind him.

These long-service professional swordsmen and engineers were all Roman citizens by birth, brothers of the voters whom Cæsar had managed in the Comitia. They also needed managing, and it was because he under-

stood them to the depths of their being that Cæsar could
get more out of them than any other general. Lucullus
had overworked his men to the point of mutiny; Crassus
alternately pampered and scolded his until they abandoned him to a shameful death; Pompeius made himself
beloved, but at the cost of being so gentle that his army
did less than its best. Cæsar alone could try his men to
the uttermost and stop just before they broke. His troops
endured tremendous losses, not only on the battlefield
but by forced marches and starvation; and the survivors
adored him.

But the breaking-point was always there, a menace
in the background. The Romans conquered the world
partly because they were brave, partly because they
obeyed orders; yet they knew that what they had under-
taken was an almost superhuman task, and sometimes
they were ready to panic at the possibility of failure.
When all prisoners of war automatically became the
slaves of their captors there was no temptation to surrender; at this period all Romans, of every class, quite
genuinely preferred death to slavery. But from time to
time bodies of despairing soldiery would commit suicide
in heaps, rather than wait for inevitable death. One of
Cæsar's own legions was destroyed by despair, rather
than by the unimportant Gallic tribe which had besieged
it; but that happened in his absence, when they had
been left under a weak commander.

For though Cæsar was infallible when dealing with
troops in the mass, he occasionally made mistakes in his
choice of senior officers. Quintus Titurius Sabinus may

have been forced on him as a political nominee, like
Quintus Cicero, brother of the orator; but he should
never have been given such a responsible post. It is interesting to note that the only one of Cæsar's officers who
would not follow him in the Civil War was his second
in command, Labienus. He must have disliked his commander throughout the Gallic campaigns which he did
so much to win; yet Cæsar never noticed it.

But in April 58 all this lay in the future. The legion
at Geneva, and the other five legions collecting in Roman Gaul, knew only that the professional politician
who had come from Rome to command them had turned
aside a threatened barbarian invasion. That was a spirited
action, but then the holder of a Civic Crown must be
personally courageous. Yet he was by trade a party-boss,
given this command as a reward for political services;
soon they would resume the ordinary round of garrison
duty, while he amassed a great fortune from the suitors
in the law courts.

The Helvetii were still set on migration to the west,
and their march put all Gaul in a ferment. On the upper
Saone lived the Ædui, one of the strongest and most
civilized of the Gallic tribes, who a generation ago had
deliberately chosen to enroll themselves among the allies of Rome. Faced with an invasion of the Helvetii,
they appealed to Cæsar for help.

Similar appeals had been made in the past, and ignored. Once a Roman governor began interfering in
tribal affairs, it was difficult to see where he would stop;
the Ædui, for all their protestations of friendship, gave

nothing to Rome, and no return was due to them. But
Cæsar decided on a forward policy.

It is difficult to see why. His excellent book tells us
what he did, but he never gives his reasons for doing it.
The conventional, and cynical, explanation is that he
wanted to win great victories and increase his fame so
that one day he should surpass Pompeius; in fact, that he
wanted a war and did not care who was the enemy. But
Cæsar's whole record shows that he was reluctant to
shed Roman blood. He must have known that to protect
the Ædui would inevitably lead to the conquest of all
Gaul. His troops would suffer heavy loss, and there
would be no plunder of value, as the barbarian enamels
of Gaul, though we admire them in our museums, were
not esteemed in Rome.

It seems to me, though this is only conjecture, that
Cæsar deliberately made up his mind that the civilized
world would be enriched by the addition of Gallic tribes.
In the east Rome ruled great cities, inhabited by spirit-
less Levantines; in Africa and Spain she ruled untamed
barbarians, hostile and savage. But the Gauls, though un-
civilized, were capable of civilization. We know as a
fact that within a generation Gallic soldiers were the
mainstay of the legions, and that Gaul quickly became
a happier and richer version of the Italian countryside.
It is possible that Cæsar foresaw what would come.

For whatever reason, Cæsar led six legions into the
land of the Æduans. The army campaigned for ten
years, and did not return until all Gaul had been conquered.

When they saw Roman troops in their land some
Æduans wished to make common cause with the Helvetii, and as Cæsar's only horse were local mercenaries of
doubtful loyalty he followed the invaders with caution;
until presently they turned on him.

A hand-to-hand fight with Gauls was always a near
thing for Roman troops. Man for man they were smaller,
and they could not forget that in the past many Roman
armies had been destroyed by the same foe; fifty years
earlier these same Helvetii had killed a Consul and
wiped out the army he led. Cæsar had six legions, probably 30,000 foot; but he considered the foe more numerous. He drew up his men with the possibility of defeat in mind. Four veteran legions held the front and
the two legions of recruits were in reserve; he himself
dismounted, and he made all his officers do the same,
to show the men that all ranks faced victory or death.
When the Helvetii rushed into a cloud of Roman javelins, their first charge was held, and Cæsar knew that
the day was won; for barbarians, unlike civilized troops,
could never reorganize after a check. But as the Romans
advanced, the enemy reserve took them in flank, and
Cæsar had to maneuver his force to fight on two fronts,
the two legions of the second line facing to the right.
(How did the Romans pass orders among such a throng
of excited men, all shouting their war cries, and with all
the officers dismounted so that they could not be identi-
fied from a distance?)

The Helvetii were slowly pushed back to their fortified camp, and after dark, at the end of a long day's

fighting, the Romans stormed it. The barbarians fled
blindly eastward. But the Romans were too exhausted
to pursue, and did not trust their hired cavalry; so the
enemy got away without further loss. But now the
peasants of the countryside knew which was the winning
side, and the losers were so harried by local levies that
they offered complete submission if only they might de-
part unmolested. Cæsar firmly sent them back to their
old home, which he wished to see occupied; for empty
farms on the Roman frontier were a standing invitation
to German raiders.

As anyone might have foretold, after Cæsar had pro-
tected the Ædui there was no going back. The Sequani,
neighbors and lifelong enemies of the Ædui, had called
in an army of German mercenaries. King Ariovistus and
a constantly growing horde of German warriors had been
quartered in eastern Gaul for the last twenty years, op-
pressing their employers as well as their enemies. Cæsar
curtly ordered them to return across the Rhine; Ariovistus at first tried to argue, but when he understood that
the Romans were in earnest he accepted the challenge—
and the Roman army must make another forward bound
to occupy the Sequanian fortress of Besançon before the
Germans held it.

Cæsar's men very nearly mutinied when they learned
that they were to fight Germans, even bigger and fiercer
men than Gauls; and all to defend a misty barbarian village more than a hundred miles beyond the edge of the
civilized world. Cæsar handled the unrest with a mas-
terly touch. He announced that he personally would

march against Ariovistus, and that the Tenth Legion, the best corps in his army, would certainly follow; the others might fight or run away, just as they pleased.

Cæsar's skill in handling nervous troops was unrivaled, but it was not exactly due to the sympathy of a fellow soldier. His book, our only authority for these events, shows the state of his feelings. The common soldiers are always "our men," never referred to by any warmer expression; he took pains to see that they were adequately fed and punctually paid, and heavy casualties distressed him. But "our men" must do what they are told, or suffer severe punishment; and he no more hides his contempt for their occasional cowardice than his proprietary pride in their more usual gallantry; they are creatures of a lesser breed, brought into the world to obey the orders of noble Roman magistrates.

After a fruitless attempt at negotiation, in which, distrusting his Gallic horse, he formed a cavalry escort from men of the Tenth Legion mounted on Gallic ponies, Cæsar led his whole army against the German camp; for Ariovistus would not come out to fight, as his soothsayers told him that this was an unlucky month for Germans. To storm a fortified camp held by an unbeaten enemy was notoriously a hazardous undertaking, but Cæsar's army accomplished it. At the only moment when things looked doubtful Publius Crassus, son of the Triumvir, ordered up the reserves on his own responsibility. Young Crassus, who commanded the Gallic horse, was of course himself mounted; but again we must wonder how the Romans managed to pass orders down a formation which must have been three thousand yards long.

Myriads of Germans were slain in the assault. Ariovistus escaped across the Rhine with a handful of followers; but both his wives were killed in the sack, and his army never again bothered the Romans.

In two distinct campaigns Cæsar had destroyed two dangerous enemies. His reputation as a general was established. When we recall that his only previous military experience had been as a volunteer at the storming of Mytilene and as commander in minor police operations in Spain, we can measure the extent of his achievement. Just before his forty-second birthday he found himself leading an army of 30,000 men, through roadless and unmapped country, against an enemy of much greater strength who had often beaten Roman armies in the past. He maneuvered his thousands among mountains and forests as though they were a squad on the parade ground; though he must depend on untrustworthy native horse he always knew what the enemy were doing, and his men never went hungry. He won his first two battles by hard fighting, without tactical finesse; but his men fought so well because they were superbly managed, in camp and on the march, by a great general who was also a great administrator, a great quartermaster, and a great statesman.

It was now autumn, the time for him to return to home politics. He quartered his army for the winter in Besançon, far to the north of the old frontier of Roman

Gaul, and hastened across the Alps to pick up the threads of City affairs from his Cisalpine province. For if he entered Rome his commission as pro-Consul automatically expired; it would be nine years before he saw the City again, and then he came to abolish its domestic politics.

These domestic politics were then in even greater confusion than usual. Clodius, the gang-leader who had been left to manage the Comitia, was completely out of hand and was threatening his employers. He had enjoyed beating up the Lictors of Bibulus; he repeated the performance with the Lictors of Aulus Gabinius, Consul for 58, though Gabinius had been elected as a nominee of the Triumvirs. When Pompeius intervened to protect his creature, Clodius dared to turn on the great man himself. The unfortunate Pompeius had muddled himself into a thoroughly false position. At first glance he seemed the most important man in Rome, and it was assumed that he was responsible for every action of the government. But he could not control the Senate, he had no military force, and now he had lost his majority in the Comitia. Clodius openly threatened him with lynching if he thwarted the will of the people, and Clodius had beaten up two Consuls in two successive years; Pompeius was genuinely afraid, so afraid that during the autumn he ceased to attend the Senate.

In exile the farsighted Cicero began to think of a future alliance between Pompeius and the Optimates. But many things must be forgiven and forgotten before the old legate of Sulla, who had changed sides to obtain the Consulship as a Popular candidate, could work in double harness with Cato and the nobility. Yet Pompeius was drifting away from Cæsar. Holding responsible posts in the army of Gaul were Quintus Cicero and young Publius Crassus; but Pompeius had no representative with Cæsar, and Julia was the only link between the two leaders.

At the beginning of the year, before Cæsar had even started for Gaul, two Prætors had made the point that all the "acts" of his Consulship were of doubtful validity because his fellow Consul, Bibulus, had declared them ill-omened. The powerful Triumvirate had the question adjourned indefinitely; but Cæsar had put himself legally in the wrong, and when he should become a private citizen an enemy might prosecute him. His pro-Consular command ran for four more years; something would have to be done before it ended.

The beginning of 57 saw a fresh grouping of forces in the riotous Comitia. Clodius was now too outrageous to be endured. He had originally been patronized by the Triumvirs because only he could get a verdict against the eloquence of Cicero; the obvious remedy was to bring back Cicero to cope with him. But this needed a vote from the Comitia, which Clodius controlled. Pompeius, the great soldier, could think of no better way of dealing with him than to set up a rival gang-leader to oppose him in the Forum. During the summer a second gang appeared, financed by Pompeius and led by the Tribune Titus Annius Milo. They fought it out with clubs and fists in the streets and in the Forum, while no laws could be passed and Cicero waited nervously at Brindisi for his promised pardon.

Meanwhile the new campaigning season opened, and Cæsar returned to his army, still quartered at Besançon in central Gaul. He brought with him two more legions recruited in Cisalpine Gaul, making a total force of eight legions or about 40,000 regular Roman foot.

The Gauls never united to fight the Romans in a body, and in fact each tribe was divided into Roman and anti-Roman factions. The barbarians appreciated the amenities of civilization which only Rome could give them; but they did not like regular taxation and orders from above, the price of entering the world-state. Most tribes were willing to pay a small tribute, send a few hostages, and supply a contingent of cavalry; but they would not put up with a garrison of Roman soldiers living permanently in their land, levying forced contributions of grain for rations and pinching the bottoms of their women. At first the Ædui rejoiced to be free of their oppressive German allies; but they were dismayed when the Romans settled down in Besançon for an indefinite stay, instead of taking the proffered tribute and going home to the old province.

While the Romans remained in their fortified capital the Ædui could do nothing; but their neighbors to the north determined to halt the advance. These northerners formed the great confederation of the Belgæ, related tribes of mixed Gallic and German culture; they held all the country from the Seine to the mouth of the Rhine, and had begun to settle in southern Britain. United, they would be by far the strongest force in Gaul; but they were seldom united.

Cæsar broke up their cumbrous and slow-moving advance by the marching speed of his disciplined army. Without waiting for a pretext he led seven legions to the land of the nearest Belgian tribe, the Remi. The enormous Belgian host, 300,000 strong, was drifting south; but the Remi found themselves unsupported in the presence of the main Roman army. Without inquiring into the reason for this unprovoked invasion, they offered complete submission. Cæsar was in fact attacking his neighbors for the simple and savage reason that they were too weak to defend themselves; but while he behaved with the unscrupulous greed of a German war chief he expected the niceties of civilized diplomacy from the barbarians who negotiated with him. There were honest men in the Senate who recognized this double-dealing and were ashamed of it; but as they were also members of the Optimate party their protests could be disregarded as factious opposition.

When the main force of the Belgians lumbered up to the river Aisne, the Romans lined the bank; after some bloody skirmishing the barbarians withdrew, chiefly because they were short of food. But no pitched battle had been fought, and the Belgians did not consider themselves beaten.

More Belgians now offered tribute and hostages, on the implied condition that the Romans should go away. But the Nervii, the proudest warriors in the confederation, remained defiant. They had withdrawn to their own territory north of the Sambre, where they could not harm the Romans; but they announced that a Roman invasion would be resisted, and Cæsar chose to treat this example of elementary self-respect as an unprovoked act of aggression.

He led his army straight into their land, and was very nearly beaten for his pains. The barbarians, at home in thorny swamps which baffled not only the Romans but their auxiliaries from the more open lands of southern Gaul, brought off a successful ambush of the main Roman column of march. As the van was halting to make camp the enemy suddenly streamed down from wooded hilltops; the soldiers at once fell in under the nearest standard; but many of them were without armor, for on long marches the men wore tunics, carrying their mail in a bundle.

For a few minutes it was touch and go whether the Roman line would break. African archers, hired Gallic horse, and in general all the non-Roman light troops attached to the army fled before the Nervian charge. The Romans, with 35,000 foot in line, were outnumbered, so the battle must have sprawled up and down the wooded trail; in the confusion some Nervians penetrated the half-built trenches of the Roman camp, and panic-stricken followers increased the chaos by fleeing at random, sometimes toward other groups of the enemy. On the left flank the Ninth and Tenth Legions advanced victoriously, while the Eighth and Eleventh in the center held their ground; but on the right the Twelfth and Seventh were in grave trouble; the Twelfth in particular, with most of its centurions dead, was clubbed in a dense mass; the standard of one cohort fell into enemy hands, and the whole legion was very near breaking up.

Cæsar had been riding with his favorite Tenth Legion; when he saw that all was going well on their front he left them under the command of Labienus, his most trusted legate, and galloped off to put things right where the Twelfth were in difficulties; dismounting, he seized a shield from a rear-rank man and himself led a charge on foot. Roman officers did not normally carry shields because they were not supposed to fight hand-to-hand; and Cæsar was not only the commander in chief but a pro-Consul who two years ago had been official and ceremonial head of the state. His personal courage was never questioned; but, courage apart, it was a remarkable physical achievement for a man of forty-three whose youth had scandalized Rome by its luxury and debauchery. The Twelfth responded, pushing back the enemy to gain room to fight. Then Labienus, having scattered the foe on his front, brought up his two legions to take the main body of the barbarians in flank.

The Nervii were stubborn, proud of their reputation as the best warriors in Gaul. While a way remained open they would not retreat, and after they had been surrounded they died rather than yield. Next day the old men of the tribe, who had hidden with the women among the marshes of the Scheldt, sent in their submission; they explained that they could not continue the struggle, for their army was reduced from 60,000 men to 500, and from a tribal council of 600 only three nobles were left.

These were the kind of people every Roman admired. Cæsar took pains to treat them well; not only did he leave them in possession of their lands but he reminded neighboring tribes that they were now under Roman protection, and that these lands must not be raided though all their guardian warriors were slain.

But that was the end of the Nervii. It seems a pity, for they were an interesting people, who have been forgotten only because their historians could not write. Cæsar relates that in their heyday they forbade foreign traders to sell them what they considered unmanly luxuries, more particularly wine. They were determined to be the bravest warriors in Gaul, and they succeeded in their ambition. If only the lament their bards chanted after this great battle had come down to us it would seem as stirring as any poem about Spartans at Thermopylæ.

Every soldier in the Roman army remembered that desperate fight for the rest of his life. Cæsar was always glad to meet a fellow veteran of the great day, and treasured the cloak he put on after the crucial counterattack. One might even say that he displayed chivalry in his kindness to the gallant losers. But chivalry was not in general a Roman virtue, and before that summer was out he had shown the ruthless, cold-blooded severity which was the least pleasant aspect of his character.

The Atuatuci were a small tribe of Germans who had crossed over to the western, or Gallic, side of the Rhine;

they were members of the Belgian alliance, and their
army had been marching to join the Nervii when the
great battle was fought. They at once retired to their
principal fortress, and when Cæsar arrived and prepared
to besiege it they opened negotiations for surrender.

The negotiations were concluded just as the Romans
finished building a moving siege-tower which could over-
top the barbarian ramparts. The terms were that the
Atuatuci should hand over their arms and admit the Romans to their fortress; the Romans would then protect
them from their enemies. But on the night of the surrender some warriors repudiated their rulers and made
a sudden attack on the Roman lines. They had buried
their swords rather than surrender them, and these they
produced from their hiding-places; but for shields they
used improvised pieces of wickerwork covered with
cloth, which proves that the rendition of arms had been
carried out in good faith.

During Cæsar's own lifetime Consul had fought
fellow Consul, Lucullus had made war when the Senate
ordered peace, and Sulla had led his rebellious army into
Rome. He must have known very well that even civilized states cannot always control their soldiery. But he
chose to apply to hysterical barbarians a higher standard
of public morality than his own City displayed. He
claimed that the Atuatuci had forfeited all claim to quarter by making a treacherous attack after their rulers had
surrendered. When his men had captured the flimsy
little town, killing 4,000 defenders in the process, he
sold all the survivors as slaves, men, women, and chil-

dren. They were 53,000 souls, and that was the end of the Atuatuci.

Meanwhile Publius Crassus had led one legion on a triumphal progress westward to the Atlantic coast. Every tribe he encountered submitted without resistance. Cæsar might boast that he had conquered the whole of Gaul, from the Rhine to the Pyrenees. He reported as much to the Senate, who ordered a thanksgiving lasting fifteen days, an unprecedented recognition; no previous public thanksgiving had lasted for more than ten days.

Cæsar then stationed his army in winter-quarters along the Loire, and himself returned to Cisalpine Gaul.

That year the confusion in Rome was worse than ever. Milo, the new gangster, might sometimes check Clodius in the Comitia (in January one of their faction fights choked the sewers of Rome with corpses), but only Cicero could rally the Senate against him. So in September Pompeius arranged that Cicero should return from exile; and Cicero, with prompt gratitude, sponsored a law to give Pompeius special powers to oversee the corn supply. It was just the kind of special extraordinary office that satisfied Pompeius's craving for honorary distinction; he was to enjoy supreme command in any province he visited, and in general he was granted the sort of roving commission he had earlier held against the pirates.

The corn supply of the City needed an overseer, for famine threatened. Pompeius quickly put things to rights, with the competence that more than outweighed his overweening vanity. Although it was the Roman custom to

lay up all shipping at the approach of winter, he personally visited Sicily and Sardinia at the height of the
autumn storms and persuaded the corn merchants to get
their cargoes moving out of season. In Rome the price of
bread fell immediately, and Pompeius enjoyed a brief
spell of popularity.

To so experienced a political observer as Cicero it
looked as though the Triumvirate was breaking up. So
far Crassus had got nothing out of the deal, though he
had paid the enormous debts of his colleagues; and
Cæsar and Pompeius, who were each in his own way
satisfied, could not agree on the question of whether the
undoubted usefulness of Clodius outweighed his undoubted rascality. Cicero began to back Pompeius against
Crassus, who retorted by threatening to loose Clodius on
him. It had often been demonstrated in the past that two
rulers in Rome meant civil war; it was time for Cæsar to
straighten things out.

Cæsar therefore called a conference at Lucca, within
the southern boundary of his province of Cisalpine Gaul.
There in the spring of 56 the Triumvirs assembled their
supporters, partly to demonstrate to the Optimates that
they were too strong to be overthrown. There arrived
two hundred Senators, and magistrates enough to bring
two hundred Lictors, a gathering such as had never been
seen before in any provincial town. Arrangements were
made for the future as openly as at a modern party con-
vention. There was no longer any pretense that the Triumvirate was a mere gathering of like-minded men; it
was nakedly the government of Rome.

Cæsar was granted Gaul for another five years, until March 49, with the right to increase his army to ten legions; in 48 he was to be Consul again, so his position was assured for the next eight years. Crassus and Pompeius were to be the Consuls for 55, and then each was to take a five-year pro-Consular command of the same type as Cæsar's—Pompeius in Spain and Crassus in Syria.

For Cæsar was now the talk of Rome, and his colleagues, who had once despised him as a politician of the streets, were eager to copy his exploits. He had led Roman armies to the limits of the world; he might even visit Germany and Britain, unknown even to Greek explorers. Henceforth Cæsar is the most newsworthy of the Triumvirs, though any sensible Roman would admit that the reputations of Crassus and Pompeius rested on more secure foundations, victory over civilized foes, Spartacus and Mithridates.

The famous conference at Lucca lasted only a few days, for when the three leaders had made friends again it was easy to find rewards for each of them. Then Crassus and Pompeius went back to the City, and Cæsar returned to his army for the campaigning season of 56.

The winter had been quiet, though Roman arms had suffered one check, which, curiously enough, was not avenged. Cæsar had sent his legate, Servius Sulpicius Galba, with one legion, to open a route through the Great St. Bernard Pass by pushing southward from the upper Rhone. Galba met such fierce opposition that he was compelled to withdraw northward. But the Romans were not interested in these barren Alpine valleys, whose conquest would yield no plunder. The mountaineers were left in poverty-stricken independence, an island of freedom surrounded by conquered provinces, until in the next generation the tidy-minded Augustus rectified the anomaly.

But when Cæsar thought that a barbarian tribe had anything worth taking, he judged their behavior by stricter standards. The Veneti (who lived in what is now Brittany) had offered submission to young Publius Crassus, and during the winter Roman officers had been sent to their territory to buy grain for the army. But the Veneti, untutored barbarians, misunderstood the situation. They thought that if they paid tribute the Romans would go away; that was why they had offered it. Tired of Roman officers who proposed to stay all winter, they suddenly arrested two of them and chained them in a dungeon.

Cæsar took this as a declaration of war. But the campaign needed lengthy preparation, for the Veneti were a queer folk. They were seafaring barbarians, an unusual combination. It is hard to understand the object of their seafaring; they traded with Britain, but Britain had a slightly more backward form of the common culture of Gaul, and one would not expect that in either country there would be a keen demand for the products of the other. However, the Veneti, at home on the sea, made seafaring pay; and for their trade they built the most remarkable ships.

Roman warships were galleys moved by oars; but these Gallic warships were fitted with stout masts and

sails of leather; their hulls were of oak, taller and stouter
than the hulls of any vessel which sailed the sheltered
waters of the Mediterranean; everything was constructed
for strength, though it brought increased weight; even
the standing rigging and the anchor cables were thick
iron chain.

The Veneti reared their fortresses on the headlands
of narrow peninsulas, with the sea on three sides; very
often the entrance was passable only at low tide, and Romans, men of the tideless inland sea, could not calculate
in advance the ebb and flow.

As it was too dangerous for the army to besiege these
seaports, the only thing to do was to build a fleet, and
Cæsar ordered his men to do so. At the mouth of the
Loire the soldiers sat down and carried out their orders,
as that army of craftsmen would have carried out an
order to build a city or dig a canal. When the fleet was
built, apparently in a few weeks, trained sailors were
fetched from the Mediterranean; but they were only
rare technical experts, whose job was to teach the soldiers how to row; the versatile foot of those wonderful
legions would act as marines, to capture enemy vessels by
boarding.

So eventually it fell out. The fleets met in battle
within a deep Breton bay, with the Roman army watching from the shore. At first the Veneti had the better of
it; their towering sailing-ships were too solid to take hurt
from the beaks of light Roman galleys, and while they
kept on the move soldiers could not board them; the
Gauls from their high forecastles harassed the crowded

rowers with arrows and javelins. The watching army feared to see their fleet destroyed before their eyes, and cultured Romans called to mind the anguish of the Athenians at Syracuse. In the nick of time the wind dropped; the Venetian sailing-ships were becalmed, but the Roman galleys moved more easily than before. They took the enemy in detail, boarding one ship at a time in overwhelming numbers. By nightfall the Venetian navy had been destroyed.

No mercy was granted to the Veneti. All their nobles were executed, and the rest of the population was sold into slavery. Gaul shuddered at the revenge Rome exacted for the imprisonment of two officers. Cæsar put it all down in his book, without comment. He liked the Gauls, and believed they were capable of assimilating Roman civilization; but a defeated foe possessed no rights.

About the same time his legate Quintus Titurius Sabinus conquered Normandy, and Publius Crassus pushed southward to the western Pyrenees. All Gaul was undoubtedly subdued, and next year Cæsar might invade some unexplored land, Britain or Germany.

In Rome rumors of a projected invasion of Britain caused great excitement, for Britain was completely unknown. In southern Gaul were merchants who had traded there, but their accounts of the mysterious island varied; presumably some thought it would be good for business if Britain were annexed; these exaggerated the value of the pearl-fishery and revived gossip about gold mines in the west, mines that had been worked out cen-

turies before. Others considered Britain a valuable market which they wished to keep to themselves; they hoped
to discourage Cæsar by telling him that the north was
inhabited by savage hunters who grew no corn. This was
as untrue as the tales of pearl-fishing, but Cæsar could
not check his information. In his book he put down
everything he was told. The resulting picture is incon-
sistent with itself, and modern archæology has shown it
to be wholly inaccurate; but Cæsar's *Gallic War* has
such a reputation for veracity (and rightly) that his false
description of Britain still appears in some modern text-
books.

All the same, though Romans talked excitedly of the
marvelous exploits of Cæsar, Cicero's letters prove that
at this time Pompeius was considered the real ruler of
the City. The Triumvirate had been patched up at
Lucca, but it was seen as an alliance between a great
man and two useful subordinates. Next in importance to
Pompeius came Crassus, with Cæsar lying third; this
was made plain by the arrangements for next year, 55.
Pompeius and Crassus were to be Consuls while Cæsar
remained in the north.

But the distinguished soldier and the able man of
business were between them unable to control the tur-
bulent City. Prominent Senators might be threatened
with the fate of Cicero, exile on a trumped-up charge;
the populace could not be frightened by threats, nor
could they be bribed to vote for the two Triumvirs,
who were regarded by the lower classes as Optimates at
heart. Cato was back from Cyprus to lead the opposition

in the Senate, and young Lucius Domitius Ahenobarbus, a Senator of very noble birth who would have held a Consulship in 55 if these great men had not run for office out of turn, was brave enough, and rich enough, to lead his own rioters against Clodius and the boys.

A farcical situation continued throughout the autumn of 56. The Triumvirs, who could divide among themselves the legions and provinces of the Roman world, could not get themselves elected by the Comitia. But they were strong enough to stop the election of anyone else; every meeting was adjourned, amid bloody rioting, without coming to a decision. This continued until January 55, when the old Consuls laid down their office. As no successors had been elected, the constitution provided that elections must be held at once, under the presidency of an Interrex.

Pompeius lost patience. He appealed to the veterans of his war against Mithridates, now farming peacefully all over Italy; for the special January election enough of them visited Rome to carry the two Triumvirs into office. They came unarmed, but it was one of the most disorderly elections ever held in Rome; Cato was wounded, and many other citizens were killed. Before the veterans had time to go home the other arrangements of Lucca were forced through the Comitia; Cæsar got his five-year extension of command, Pompeius had Spain for five years also, and Crassus Syria, with command in the war against Parthia.

So ended a year which had seen the Roman dominions greatly extended and the City itself a prey to an-

archy. It is important to remember that the constitution
Cæsar eventually overthrew had already proved itself
unworkable, for that is his chief justification.

Now that all Gaul had submitted, Cæsar looked round
for another land to invade; but the barbarians took the
initiative and he had first to defend his gains. Rumors
had spread eastward that the Gauls had been overthrown
by an invader from the south, and the tribes of west
Germany moved quickly to get their share of any loot
that might be going. During the winter two German
peoples, the Usipetes and the Tencteri, had crossed the
lower Rhine into what is now southern Holland; they
claimed to be fugitives, defeated by the Suebi and look-
ing for a safe refuge; but they were in fact moving in to
take advantage of the destruction of the military power
of the Nervii. Cæsar marched down the Meuse to com-
pel them to withdraw.

The Germans tried to negotiate. They offered to hold
their new lands as allies of the Roman people, or to move
on to any other part of Gaul which Cæsar might assign
to them. But they would fight where they stood rather
than return to Germany. Cæsar made a counter offer.
The Ubii, a tribe living east of the Rhine, had appealed
to him for help against the same Suebi who were the
enemies of these refugees; let the Usipetes and Tencteri
go back to the land of the Ubii, who would rent farms
to such valuable reinforcements. The German envoys
replied that they must report this new offer to their
chiefs; this would take three days, and in the meantime
it would be prudent for Cæsar to halt, to avert the dan-

ger of an accidental clash if his army met the German
outposts.

If the Usipetes and Tencteri were genuinely seeking
a peaceful refuge this request was reasonable. But Cæsar
picked up a rumor that they were only trying to delay
him until their scattered raiding parties had returned to
the main body; he could not really know the truth, for
in the same section of his book he points out that the
gossip of Gallic newsmongers was of no value as evidence. But he continued his advance.

When the German envoys returned, three days later,
the Roman army was only seven miles from the barbarian
camp. The envoys begged for an immediate halt; let the
Roman van stand fast for three more days while mes-
sengers rode to the Ubii to confirm their offer and to
inspect the land proposed for settlement. This again was
a reasonable suggestion. But there were envious Gauls
to whisper that the raiding horsemen of the Usipetes
were riding home at speed; and that the suggested stand-
still was only a ruse to gain time.

In Cæsar's place an honorable commander might have
done one of two things. He might have granted the
German request, halted his men, and continued the negotiations, on the assumption that these Germans were
genuinely in flight from the Suebi, and that what they
sought was a land where they might live in peace. Or
he might have sent back the envoys, telling them that
the Roman army had orders to remove all Germans to
the eastern bank of the Rhine, and that unless they
wanted a war they must begin their retreat at once. The

Usipetes and Tencteri were evidently afraid of the Romans; probably they would have retreated.

Cæsar did neither one thing nor the other, and such a great soldier cannot be excused on the ground that he was dithering, with his mind still undecided. He told the German envoys to come back next day, bringing with them as many of their leading chiefs as possible; thus they could settle the Ubian business without referring it back for ratification. But he sent his van forward, with orders to occupy a position only three miles from the German camp. This position had considerable military importance, for in it was a good supply of clean water, rare in that marshy land. Cæsar's van was made up of 5,000 hired Gallic cavalry; they were bad troops, disobedient and unsteady; but they hated Germans, and the enemy could muster only 800 horse to face them.

As Cæsar must have foreseen, the 800 Germans rode out to clear the environs of their camp, which contained their families and all their possessions. He may not have foreseen what happened next; 800 Germans charged 5,000 Gauls, and routed them. Fugitives came tumbling into the legionary camp, and Cæsar gave orders that the whole Roman army should advance next morning.

The legions had only eight miles to march, and they took the Germans by surprise. On the way they encountered the envoys and chiefs, coming to resume negotiations; by German standards yesterday's skirmish was not important, and there had been no declaration of war. Once again, Cæsar should either have halted to parley, or sent back the ambassadors. Instead he arrested them, marched up to the barbarian camp, and stormed it easily in face of a leaderless defense. The Gallic horse, smarting from shameful defeat, hunted down the German women and children; and when the barbarian army broke, the fugitives found themselves trapped between their pursuers and the Rhine. On that morning the Usipetes and Tencteri made up 430,000 souls, and by evening they had been wiped out. When Cæsar offered to free their ambassadors they begged to remain in his camp, as now they had no kin to return to.

This ghastly massacre delighted the Gauls, who held that the only good German was a dead German. The legions also were pleased with their plunder, gained at the cost of a few dozen wounded. But when the news reached Rome, men of honor were genuinely shocked. Cæsar had attacked while ambassadors were actually in his camp seeking peace. In the Senate Cato advocated the ancestral method of dealing with a dishonorable commander; let Cæsar be handed over, bound, to his enemies, that they might choose his punishment. (But Cæsar had no *surviving* enemies.) Of course the proposal was voted down, and Cæsar was thanked by the Senate for his spirited defense of the Gallic allies of Rome.

The Romans were a tough people, as willing to inflict death as to endure it. We must remember that the voters in the Comitia were not the parasitical mob of the later Empire; many were veterans, and the rest would take the chance of a cracked skull behind Clodius or

Milo for the fun of it, or for quite a small bribe. But to wipe out a community of more than 400,000 men, women, and children was something outside the common run of experience. Henceforth Cæsar's reputation for ruthless, bloodthirsty cruelty was firmly established, among his friends as among his enemies. Throughout the later civil wars he repeatedly offered quarter; but his fellow citizens died sword in hand rather than trust the mercy of a man who had massacred all those helpless Germans. Morals apart, and morally it was a beastly business, the slaughter of the Usipetes and Tencteri was a blunder; a politician whose enemies cannot trust his offers of pardon can never bring peace to his country.

55 was altogether a bad year for Cæsar. The rest of the summer was taken up with his first expedition to Britain, a carelessly prepared raid which might have ended in disaster but for the high morale and imperturbable courage of the legionaries. But then they owed their high morale to three years of victory under Cæsar; perhaps the episode should be regarded as another example of his faculty of getting the utmost from his men, easing the strain just before breaking-point was reached.

While at Boulogne a small fleet was prepared, he led his army up the Rhine to the region of Cologne and ordered a bridge to be built. This was all in the day's work for Roman soldiers, and in ten days they had felled standing timber, trimmed it into planks and beams, and constructed a trestle bridge which from Cæsar's own description must have been remarkably like the Bailey

bridges used by the allied armies in the Second World
War. Apparently every man in his army was not only a
carpenter but a natural engineer who knew by instinct
where every strut should go. Cæsar then marched into
Germany, where he remained for eighteen days, chal-
lenging the Germans to turn him out. As no hostile
army appeared, he then returned to Gaul. But this was
more than pointless bravado. He had crossed into the
territory of the Ubii, the German tribe who had offered
alliance to Rome; and he had raided the land of their
foes the Sugambri. It was a hint that Rome was an ally
of value, and that no part of the world was beyond the
reach of her armies.

The news of this first venture of a Roman army in
the lands east of the Rhine made a great sensation when
it reached the City, though it was soon overshadowed
by the much more exciting news that Cæsar had landed
in Britain. That remote island fascinated the Romans,
who were half-inclined to regard it as the Land of the
Dead, or at least as a suburb of Hades. In Britain lay
the headquarters of the Druid organization, which also
flourished in Gaul; and the Druids were mysterious
necromancers. At the beginning of the *Gallic Wars*
Cæsar describes Druidism at length, and if his description were correct it should have been a powerful secret
society binding together all the Celtic tribes; but as in
fact the course of the Roman conquest proves that nothing bound together all the Celtic tribes, and the Druids
never appear in the later part of his story, we must con-
clude that Cæsar was misinformed on this aspect of bar-

barian life, as he was on many others. Druids were an interesting topic for religious speculation, but of no importance in civil or military affairs.

Cæsar ventured into Britain with only two legions, carried in eighty ships. A small force of Gallic horse were supposed to join him, sailing from another harbor; but their ships were scattered by a storm, and they never reached him. He coasted by the chalk cliffs of the Channel to the marshes of Kent, where local tribesmen gathered on the beach to dispute his landing. The invasion nearly ended before it had begun, for the legionaries shrank from jumping into waist-deep water in face of a hostile army. But the veteran who carried the sacred Eagle of the Tenth Legion, leaping into the waves, began to wade ashore with it; and the men had to follow or be eternally disgraced by the loss of their Eagle. That was a well-known device of Roman tactics, though sometimes it might fail of its effect. Suetonius relates that twice in his life Cæsar tried to rally retreating troops by compelling the Eagle-bearer to halt; one man escaped by threatening his commander with the sharp spike at the bottom of the standard-pole; the second just pushed the Eagle into Cæsar's arms and went on running.

However, on this occasion the dodge worked, and the Tenth Legion splashed into battle. The local inhabitants soon fled, and the Romans established their camp above the beach where their ships were drawn up.

At this time southeastern Britain was ruled by an aristocracy of Belgian nobles, who had crossed the Channel barely a generation ago. They kept up a connection with their homeland, for Commius, a chief of the Atrebates (near Arras), who on this occasion was principal scout for the Roman army, later broke with Rome and died ruling another branch of his tribe in Hampshire. Although the Belgians had migrated so recently, they had not brought their horses with them; in Britain horses big enough to carry an armed man were rare, and the nobles went to war in chariots drawn by a pair of ponies. A few war chariots met Cæsar on the beach, but there were not many nobles in that part of Kent. The Romans enjoyed a few days of relative security before the strength of the Belgians could muster from their chief centers in Hertfordshire and Essex, north of the lower Thames.

Local tribes sent envoys to the Roman camp, offering tribute on the usual terms: that the Romans should go right away and cease to bother them. When disaster struck, these envoys were within the Roman lines, and they at once reported it to their tribes. What had happened was a frequent occurrence when Mediterranean sailors tried to cope with the Atlantic; Cæsar's shipmasters had forgotten to allow for the spring tide that comes with each full moon. The ships floated off the beach, and those at anchor broke their cables. It seemed that Cæsar's two legions were stranded in Britain, with no winter stores, no communications, and no base.

Luckily it was harvest time, and Cæsar sent out parties to reap the ripe barley. The rest of the army repaired the damaged ships. They had no metal, but timber could be cut; the twelve most damaged ships were sacrificed and their nails and bronze fitments used to repair others. To men who had bridged the Rhine in ten days all this would be nothing difficult.

Then the Britons attacked in full force, as Cæsar had expected. After hard fighting they were beaten off, but an army made up entirely of infantry found the war chariots formidable foes. Each chariot carried two men, which meant that the passenger might wear heavy armor and yet come fresh to the fight; he would suddenly leap from his chariot to fight on foot, and when things grew hot his charioteer would whisk him away to safety. The chariots in the British rear guard made pursuit unrewarding.

In his writings Cæsar makes a great point of these formidable chariots, until one forgets that they were a second-best, and that every barbarian who could find a horse strong enough to carry him fought as a cavalier. Cæsar is piling up the excuses to explain his sudden withdrawal from Britain; if he had brought with him a few squadrons of horse he could have mastered these pony carts.

After a stay of less than three weeks the Romans sailed back to Gaul, with nothing accomplished. Cæsar's account of the expedition is a masterpiece of prose; the impression of Roman courage and success is so vivid that the Senate, after reading it, decreed twenty days of rejoicing for another great victory. But the Gallic cousins of those Britons knew better. All over Gaul it was whispered that these Romans were not, after all, invincible.

Cæsar knew that he must efface this impression of defeat as quickly as possible. He arranged for ships to be built in every Atlantic port of Gaul; equipment was ordered from Spain, and technical experts from the Mediterranean; though as usual most of the work was done by his soldiers. He himself designed a new pattern of ship which he thought would be better suited to the Channel; twice he had sailed to Asia, which was more naval experience than fell to the lot of most Romans; but it is also evidence of his remarkable self-confidence. His new-model transports proved just as unseaworthy as the old, but then the Romans were thoroughly inept in all maritime affairs.

Over the Alps in Rome the other two Triumvirs had blundered through their Consulship to the great pro-Consular commands arranged for them. Pompeius bought popularity by building, at his own expense, the first permanent stone amphitheater in the City (hitherto the Games had been given in temporary wooden buildings). It was opened with an unusual display, in which five hundred lions and seventeen elephants faced death; but the populace, who had no sympathy whatever with human gladiators, recognized the engaging qualities of elephants; they riotously demanded mercy for these victims; which is the sole example of kindness to animals in ancient Rome. But perhaps it was only an excuse for another riot.

Cicero had been bullied into speaking in favor of the special pro-Consular commands; he then retired temporarily from politics, and the Triumvirs faced opposition only from the eccentric Cato. With Spain Pompeius received ten legions and the right to appoint an unlimited

number of legates. He soon made it clear that he had no
intention of leaving Italy, though to retain his pro-
Consular powers he must keep outside the Pomœrium of
Rome. His legates ruled Spain for him, while his ten
legions trained between the Apennines and the Tiber.
The constitution laid it down that no permanent garrisons might remain in Italy, but of course all recruits need
training before they can march. By this device not only
the pro-Consul, but the main strength of the Spanish
field army, were available to ensure the loyalty of Rome
to the Triumvirate.

Crassus had at length attained the great command he
had sought ever since he defeated Spartacus seventeen
years before. He had ten legions and a mission to conquer Parthia. But the circumstances of his setting out
were odd and discouraging. In the first place, he had difficulty in recruiting an army. Cæsar was raising fresh
drafts for Gaul, where immortal glory and rich booty
were to be won; Pompeius, Rome's greatest soldier, was
gathering ten legions for garrison duty in civilized Spain,
with a good chance that they would in fact remain in
Italy. All recruitment was by this time voluntary, and
when the seekers of glory had gone to Gaul and the
lovers of comfort had joined the army of Spain, the army
of Syria had to take the leavings. Experienced veterans
mistrusted the legions of Crassus.

The Optimates also discouraged the enterprise. The
Tribune Caius Ateius Capito interposed his veto, point-
ing out that Parthia had never harmed Rome, and that
an invasion would be naked aggression; that was true,

but naked aggression was by now a tradition of Roman policy, and hitherto no one had objected. When Crassus went quietly on with his preparations Capito fell back on religious sanctions; as the army marched forth from the City he stood by the gate, a smoking tripod before him. He declared that this piracy must bring bad luck to Rome, and by an ancient magical formula turned back the bad luck on the soldiers themselves; let the Gods of the Underworld take down Crassus and his men to early death, sparing those unoffending Romans who remained at home. Nobody punished him for spreading alarm and despondency, which indicates the limits of the ramshackle control of internal affairs exercised by the Triumvirate.

In the following spring Cæsar set in train his second invasion of Britain. This was to be a much greater affair than the first; 600 ships were assembled, including transports for 4,000 Gallic horse. But of his ten legions he could bring only seven, for Gaul was obviously on the verge of revolt. The Treveri, one of the most warlike tribes, actually began to muster in arms, and he had to waste valuable summer weather in persuading them to disperse. He planned to take with him to Britain hostages from every important tribe; here again his plans miscarried. Dumnorix was a chief of the Æduans, the people who for generations had been friendly to Rome; but he was a leader of the anti-Roman faction, whom Cæsar thought it prudent to keep at his headquarters. When Dumnorix was ordered to sail he protested violently; he said that he was under a tabu never to cross the sea, and

that his presence was necessary at certain religious cere-
monies in the land of the Æduans. These excuses may
have been true, but they did not convince Cæsar. Dumnorix was told he must sail; and suddenly the fact of
Roman domination, which for four years had been increasing without any definite climax, broke in full force
on his fervid Celtic imagination.

He stole away from the Roman army, riding hard for
his own country at the head of his personal guard of
Æduan nobles; overtaken by Gallic cavalry in Roman
service, he called on his companions to resist, shouting
again and again that he was a free man, a warrior of a
free tribe. His oath-bound followers sat neutral while
Cæsar's mercenaries cut him down. By taking the tribes
one at a time and playing on Gallic fear of German invasion, Cæsar had brought it about that in the fifth year
of his pro-Consular command a Gallic noble must die
to be free.

After this disquieting episode he sailed for Britain,
with five legions and 2,000 horse. Labienus, with three
legions, was left to guard the Channel coast. But Labienus was his most trusted and efficient subordinate,
and a resounding victory in Britain might frighten Gaul
into renewed submission.

Three months later Cæsar was back again, and without his resounding victory. He had killed many more
Britons than last time, but the campaign could only be
called a draw. In the first place, his fleet had suffered
heavy damage in another storm; the Romans should by
this time have learned the moods of the Channel, but

they were again taken unawares by a high tide. Then Cassivellaunus, the ruler of southeastern Britain, offered battle somewhere in the region of Canterbury. Of course Cæsar won easily, but darkness hindered pursuit (and the Romans were, as usual, short of cavalry). The Britons got away, rallying to hold the fords of the lower Thames. Again Cæsar attacked, forced a crossing, and marched to sack the capital of Cassivellaunus, somewhere near St. Albans. But the war chariots harried his outposts, and meanwhile the local levies of Kent were blockading the base where he had left his fleet. Through his kinsman Commius, Cassivellaunus patched up a peace which saved Roman prestige and did the Britons no harm. Hostages and tribute were promised, though only very little was actually paid; then the Romans went away, not to return for ninety years.

All Gaul took fresh hope, seeing that it was possible to check a Roman army. Cæsar hoped that by building fortified camps near every center of unrest he would smother the threatened revolt before it could spread; but it was Cæsar's genius which had conquered Gaul, and the average legate was not a Cæsar.

The most northerly garrison was at Atuatuca, between the Meuse and the Rhine, in the land of the unwarlike Eburones. It was made up of a legion of recruits, stiffened by half a legion of veterans, and the command was shared by two legates, Quintus Titurius Sabinus and Lucius Aurunculeius Cotta. On hearing that Cæsar had started on his usual autumn journey to

Cisalpine Gaul, the Eburones rose, led by a chief of
great skill in lying, and some skill in warfare, named
Ambiorix. After besieging the fort he opened negotiations; he informed the two legates that every other Roman garrison had already fallen; but he, Ambiorix, had
no quarrel with Romans in their proper place, and
wished to spare their lives. Let them march out to link
up with Quintus Cicero, who was now retreating from
the land of the Nervii; if they went peaceably they
would be suffered to go in peace.

The soldiers in Atuatuca were very far from home.
The recruits in particular had never seen anything like
winter on the Meuse, and the cold, the leafless forest,
the sense of isolation among countless queer barbarians
had already undermined their courage. They were half-
way to panic while the legates discussed in council the
terms offered to them; and the council of war was badly
managed, with a constant leakage of information to the
frightened rank and file. Cotta stuck to the discipline
which had made Rome great. His superior officer had
ordered him to hold Atuatuca, and he would hold it. If
Cæsar happened to be defeated and dead, that was just
too bad, but it did not justify disobedience. Sabinus completely lost his nerve. He said that if the unwarlike
Eburones attacked a Roman fort it must be because they
knew of Roman disasters all over Gaul; it was his duty
to bring back what men he could to the old Province in
the south before that also was submerged in a deluge of
triumphant barbarians. Cotta and the experienced cen-

turions were overborne by the clamor of panicky recruits, and both legates agreed to order the troops to march out.

Of course they were attacked on the march. They had to abandon their baggage, but the men stood fast in hollow square from early morning to mid-afternoon. After Cotta had been wounded, Sabinus saw Ambiorix directing the attack, and sent his interpreter to offer surrender if the Gauls would grant quarter. Ambiorix ordered the Roman commander to seek mercy in person, and Sabinus was murdered during the parley. The attack continued.

By nightfall Cotta was dead, with most of the Romans. Some stragglers escaped into the woods, and eventually carried news of the disaster to Labienus; the remainder still held together in an organized body, a remarkable display of tenacity and discipline. They cut their way back to the fort and prepared to hold its defenses.

But in the night their morale finally collapsed. Roman legionaries were very fine soldiers indeed, who could outface disaster for a long time; but when their dogged courage was at last overcome, their sensitive Mediterranean temperaments took charge and the collapse was absolute. Without waiting for the morning's attack they killed themselves, fearing torture if they should be taken alive.

This episode shows clearly that Gaul was conquered by Cæsar, not by the Roman army. Sabinus despaired before he was hurt, and Cotta fought on until his men cracked; Cæsar alone used his men to the utmost, but stopped when they had reached the limit of endurance.

The triumphant Eburones at once dashed off to besiege Quintus Cicero, while other tribes attacked Labienus. But the revolt had no time to spread farther, for Cæsar had not yet started for Cisalpine Gaul. With two legions he first relieved Cicero and then went on to link up with Labienus. The latter was the only subordinate to whom Cæsar allowed a free hand; he asked him to march toward the main army, but when Labienus replied that any movement of his would be interpreted as a retreat, encouraging more tribes to join the rising, Cæsar let him do as he thought best. Labienus was unlucky to live in an era of great generals; if he had been born in another time he would be remembered as a famous soldier.

Widespread unrest kept Cæsar in Gaul until the New Year, but great events were taking place in Rome, and in January he crossed the Alps for a flying visit. Pompeius was still in Italy, exercising at long range his pro-Consular command in Spain, and fate itself seemed to be clearing the ring for a duel between the two great rivals. Julia had died in childbirth; she received a public funeral, a very rare honor for a young woman; this was in accordance with Cæsar's policy of claiming that the Julian family were more than ordinary Romans. A faithful wife and a dutiful daughter, she had provided an unofficial link between the two leaders; now the link was severed. It seemed ominous of future rivalry that during this year Cæsar had his agents build the Basilica Æmiliana, a public hall which was too obviously his answer to the Theater of Pompeius.

But the greatest difficulty of the government was that because all three Triumvirs had taken pro-Consular commands, not one of them could enter Rome. Pompeius hovered in Italy, but Crassus was now in Syria at the head of his army. He had wasted the campaigning season in pointless raids on the rich towns beside the Euphrates; but next season he must fight a decisive battle, and for a year at least he could play no part in home politics.

The Optimates controlled the Senate of leaderless Rome. Cato attacked Cæsar's ruthless policy in Gaul, and Cicero mocked the Triumvirs, unanswered because no one could answer his eloquence. Once more efforts were made to buy him, by the offer of a good post in Spain; but he refused it, and his brother's command in Gaul was not enough to keep him friendly. He could no longer be frightened into silence, for Clodius was opposed on his chosen battlefield of the Forum by Milo's gang of Optimates.

Cæsar and Pompeius were still determined not to quarrel, though that was what every detached observer expected. Now that Cæsar needed two legions to replace the losses of Atuatuca, Pompeius lent him one which had just been recruited for service in Spain. His second legion he recruited in Transalpine Gaul; it bore the Celtic name *Alauda*, the Lark, and must have been made up mostly from Gallic tribesmen who lacked Roman citizenship. That infringed the letter of the con-

stitution, which laid down that only citizens might serve
in the legions. But Gauls might now be trusted to fight
faithfully for Rome; in the same winter Publius Crassus
set out to join his father in Syria, bringing with him
6,000 Gallic cavalry.

Early in 53 Cæsar returned to the seat of war. He
led his army to the land of the Menapians, the most
northerly district of Gaul; he then once again bridged
the Rhine and challenged the Suebi to battle. But the
Germans withdrew eastward, refusing to fight. After a
short stay Cæsar retired, breaking his bridge behind him.
Ambiorix was still at large, and must be punished.

The rest of the campaigning season was devoted to
hunting him down. He was very nearly captured by a
patrol of cavalry, and his sudden flight separated him
from his army, which then dispersed. The fugitive was
left with an escort of only four horsemen, but the Roman cavalry never quite caught up with him. These
Roman cavalry were Gallic mercenaries, and though
they could be trusted to fight for their paymasters they
may have felt the normal Celtic sympathy with anyone
who is urgently wanted by the police.

Quintus Cicero had been left in command of Cæsar's
base, the old camp at Atuatuca. There he was besieged
by the German Sugambri, who had crossed the Rhine to
pillage the land of the Eburones and then suddenly
changed sides in hope of richer booty. Cicero held out
until relieved by Cæsar, though he lost several detachments of foragers; in fact, it was a very near thing, and
Cæsar was shocked at the low morale of the troops he

relieved. Gaul was not yet safe for ordinary Roman soldiers without the advantage of a genius to command
them.

In the autumn Cæsar held a solemn assembly of
chiefs from all over Gaul, where the most important
business was the execution of Acco, chief of the Senones;
he was flogged to death, the ancient Roman penalty for
rebellion. In his book Cæsar dwells on this execution in
a way that shows it was meant to terrify the Gauls; in
fact, it angered them. Then in January 52 Cæsar was
called by very urgent business to Cisalpine Gaul, and
the insulted and revengeful chiefs had several months in
which to plot their next move.

The situation in Rome had completely changed. The
Triumvirate was ended, and only two great leaders remained, who must soon be rivals for rule over the Roman world. The destruction of the Syrian expedition is
worth relating, as showing what might happen to a bad
Roman army under a general of average ability.

The legions of Crassus had been recruited from poor
material after the best men had gone into the armies of
Cæsar and Pompeius. A winter in Syria did not improve
them, for Syria was notorious for enervating luxury.
There is here an interesting difference of opinion between ancient and modern military experts. Our present
rulers hold that if soldiers are to fight well, they need
cinemas, ice cream, hot baths, and numbers of (chaste)
young women to help them write their letters home; if
after that they still fight badly, the remedy is to send
them even more films and ice cream. The ancients

thought a soldier was weakened by soft living; chaste young women had no function in the Roman army, and too many of the other kind were considered bad for discipline. The legions of Crassus did themselves very well among the brothels of the Levant, and grumbled when their commander led them into the Mesopotamian desert.

After dropping garrisons to protect his communications, Crassus had with the Eagles 28,000 legionary foot and 8,000 auxiliary horse. The main Parthian army was on the Armenian frontier, and his advance was disputed by only 1,000 mailed lancers and 10,000 mounted archers. His auxiliary cavalry ran away as soon as the Parthians appeared; the only horse remaining were 1,000 of the Gauls whom young Publius had brought from the west.

But Crassus was not dismayed. Lucullus in Armenia had often met and defeated mounted archers. A horseman must use a very short, weak bow; but his great disability is that he cannot pick up spent arrows from the ground, and so quickly runs out of ammunition. Crassus marched on in hollow square, waiting for the enemy to shoot away their arrows.

But the Parthians brought camels loaded with arrows right into the front line. This was an innovation, only possible because a few brave men had volunteered to lead the clumsy beasts into the fray, where their drivers would be unable to defend themselves. The shower of arrows did not cease, and the sulky Roman army began to waver. Young Publius tried to clear the front by

charging the enemy lancers; his Gauls were swallowed
up in the cloud of light horse, and the only indication of
their fate was the severed head of their leader, thrown
at the feet of his father, the Roman commander.

That night Crassus led back his disheartened men to
the shelter of Carrhæ, the nearest fortified town. Lack
of provisions compelled him to continue his retreat; he
struck out northward, hoping to reach Armenia, a land
too mountainous for cavalry tactics. He had already left
4,000 wounded in the hands of the Parthians, and his
men were at breaking-point. At last he accepted the
enemy's offer of a parley, though he guessed that treachery was intended. As he rode out to the hostile lines he
spoke to a subordinate. "Tell them in Rome," he said,
"that I was murdered by treachery during a conference.
Don't tell them the truth. Don't say that I had to surrender because my soldiers wouldn't fight."

The Parthians tried to capture him, and he died sword
in hand. Then mounted archers shot down his fleeing infantry one by one. The great army of Syria had contained 40,000 men (including garrisons); they were
utterly destroyed by 11,000 barbarians. 10,000 got
back to Syria, 1,000 were taken prisoner, the rest died.
The prisoners were settled in the remote oasis of Merv,
to hold the Parthian frontier against the nomads of the
steppe. A Gallic noble of Aquitaine might have met Romans for the first time, taken service with the interesting
civilized foreigners, and found himself guarding a watch-
tower in central Asia, all within ten years. What fas-

cinating stories could have been told by the campfires of Merv!

We sometimes think of the Roman army as invincible, and of Cæsar's conquest of Gaul as a walkover. But Romans did not always beat barbarians. Crassus was a competent general, who had come to the top in competition with his equals; he brought 40,000 Romans against 11,000 barbarians, and his head became a stage property in the court theater of the Parthian king. Without Cæsar, Gaul might never have entered the civilized world.

When news reached Rome that the army which Capito had devoted to the Infernal Gods had in fact gone down to Hades, the Senate was concerned for the safety of Syria. There was no time to levy fresh legions, and reinforcements must be drawn from existing armies. But taking soldiers from a powerful general was a tricky business, for a powerful general might not obey orders. A fair solution was found, whereby Cæsar and Pompeius each contributed one legion. Pompeius, by a piece of petty artfulness, broke the spirit of the pact; he offered the legion he had already lent to Cæsar. Cæsar, with conscious rectitude, obeyed orders which could not be enforced; he sent off both legions, his own and that of Pompeius; though the unfairness of the plan was soon demonstrated when Pompeius halted them in Italy, where they remained at his disposal.

Pompeius, a widower since the death of Julia, now married Cornelia, the widow of Crassus, and took over leadership of his small personal faction. That party quickly disappeared, but all the same Pompeius was strengthened. There was now no other respectable leader for respectable men to follow. Cæsar might be liked by soldiers and barbarians, but the boy-friend of King Nicomedes, the gay and profligate Ædile, would never appeal to the middle classes.

Throughout the troubled year 53 Rome was so disorderly that it was impossible to hold the Consular elections. They were therefore postponed until January 52. Both Milo and Clodius were candidates, which ensured a lively contest. Then on the 18th of January the two gangsters met accidentally on the high road; in the fight which followed, Clodius was killed.

He had been a Popular, regarded by most people as Cæsar's agent. To give him a splendid funeral the Populars constructed an enormous pyre in the Forum. But during the burning, rioting broke out again, which did not end until many public buildings, including the Senate House, had been burned to the ground. Rome was faced with anarchy, made worse by the lack of regular magistrates; for still there had been no election. The frightened Senate met in the new Theater of Pompeius and called on Pompeius, the nearest pro-Consul, to restore order.

In what capacity should he come? That was important to any Roman, and especially important to the legal-minded Pompeius. It was proposed that he should be made Dictator; but there were practical difficulties. The normal magistracies must be filled under a Dictator, which meant elections; and elections meant more bloody and destructive rioting. Cato and Bibulus, leaders of the Optimates, proposed that the Senate should declare Pompeius sole Consul, without election; and that in addition he should still keep his pro-Consular command. This completely unconstitutional proposal was accepted. Pompeius marched his troops into Rome and restored order; and in Rome he reigned, sole Consul and pro-Consul, without a colleague, as powerful as any king.

In the race for power Cæsar was being left behind. He had been one of three equal Triumvirs, but now Pompeius stood alone. Equally important was the new alignment of parties. Pompeius had his personal political machine, and the support of the veterans who had served under him in the east; but hitherto he had been counted as on the whole a Popular, of the same party as Cæsar. Now he had been placed in power by the Optimates; a coalition of Optimates and the Pompeian group of Populars would be too strong for the left-wing followers of Cæsar.

But at the moment Cæsar had no leisure for home politics. The news that Clodius, his agent, had been murdered caused a sensation among the Gauls. They had been preparing a revolt, and now it seemed that their conqueror had been repudiated by his own people. The Carnutes suddenly massacred all the Roman traders who had settled in their capital, Orléans; and when news of this reached the Arverni of central Gaul they rose in rebellion under a chief named Vercingetorix.

Cæsar had left his field army quartered in the Seine valley and beyond; southern Gaul was the old Province, certain to remain loyal, and he relied on the Ædui, hereditary friends of Rome, to keep the center friendly. But in this crisis the Ædui stood neutral. Vercingetorix acted with great energy. In a few days he could send his colleague Lucterius to threaten the Province, while all central Gaul had joined his cause.

Cæsar at once hastened to Narbonne, in the Province now menaced by Lucterius. The rebels in central Gaul cut him off from his field army, but after strengthening the fortifications of Narbonne he collected a small force from the provincial garrisons; this little expedition literally dug its way through thick snow to the borders of the Arverni, who had thought themselves safe until summer. They recalled both Vercingetorix and Lucterius for home defense, but Cæsar dodged past them, up the Rhone valley, to his main army.

The campaign that followed is too complicated to be described in detail. Vercingetorix was a better strategist than the average barbarian war chief, and he planned to use the greater mobility of his tribesmen to wear down the armored Romans. But Vercingetorix was not undisputed King of the Gauls, and his plan failed when popular opinion compelled him to hold certain famous fortresses. Cæsar stormed them one after another, and under the inspiration of his leadership heavy mailed infantry outmarched the barefoot natives. By autumn the Ædui had joined the revolt, but Vercingetorix was shut up in the hill town of Alesia. He had 80,000 men, and the Roman army besieging him was certainly smaller. But Cæsar used the spade. He set his men to dig two lines of

trenches round the mountain, placing his camp between
them. One trench kept in the garrison of Alesia, the
other held off the relieving army from western Gaul. On
two fronts at once there was bitter hand-to-hand fighting;
again Cæsar demanded from his men their utmost effort;
but the lines just held. Presently Alesia was starving, and
Vercingetorix rode out to surrender, hoping thus to gain
mercy for his followers. If he thought that a gesture
would gain mercy for anyone, he did not know Cæsar;
Vercingetorix was put in prison, a valuable trophy for
the Triumph which must follow the conquest of Gaul;
from his large army the Æduan and Arvernian contingents were held as hostages for the loyalty of their tribes;
the rest were distributed as spoil, so that every Roman
soldier received at least one slave.

Lucterius was still at large in the southwest, but Gaul
was practically reconquered. That winter Cæsar could
turn his undivided attention to home politics, which
were getting out of hand. Pompeius had appointed as
his fellow Consul, without election, his new father-in-
law, Metellus Scipio; he had also begun to work with
the Optimates, making and breaking new laws at a great
rate. One of these new laws stated flatly that no one
might stand for the Consulship unless he came personally
to the Forum as a private citizen. Now, Cæsar's command in Gaul would end on the 1st of March 49; he
had been promised the Consulship for 48, which meant
that after the election in July 49 he would be Consul-
elect, and so technically immune from prosecution; and
the gap between March and July could have been filled

by delaying to appoint his successor, so that he remained in Gaul until relieved. But to gain the Consulship under the new law he must appear in Rome as a private citizen, and Cato had publicly threatened to impeach him for illegalities committed during his first Consulship in 59. A state prosecution, with the Optimates in power, might mean exile; unless, indeed, the penalty was death. He began to negotiate at long range, and Pompeius promised to make an exception in his case. But nothing had been settled when the last embers of the Gallic revolt called him back over the Alps for the campaigning season of 51.

This last campaign was short and brutal. The rebels under Lucterius were driven to bay in Uxellodunum, and after Cæsar had cut the water supply the town surrendered. Every man in the garrison suffered the loss of his right hand; after that he was set free to beg, a warning to all potential rebels. Lucterius, who had got away, was betrayed by his Gallic host. He was imprisoned with Vercingetorix, another ornament for the future Triumph. Other leaders were flogged to death, and in general the revolt was punished with real Roman brutality. It was said, and said by Romans, that during the nine years of the conquest a million barbarians had been killed, and another million sold into slavery.

But Cæsar took great trouble with the final settlement of his new province. Taxes were fairly imposed and honestly collected; impartial law courts dispensed a sensible code of justice; above all, service in the Roman army opened a new field to Gallic ambition. While

Rome discussed with horror Cæsar's implacable cruelty, Gaul remained faithful throughout the civil wars. Those barbarians who really preferred death to servitude had found it, in Alesia or Uxellodunum; the rest discovered that in return for abandoning the religion, the language, and the way of life of their ancestors they would be allowed to share the delights of civilization. They deemed it a good bargain, and they were right. Every generous instinct makes us wish that Vercingetorix had died free; but Gaul in the first century A.D. was a prosperous land, happier than in the days of its independence.

CHAPTER SIX

CÆSAR AND POMPEIUS

ALTHOUGH Rome had been governed by force, or the threat of it, ever since the murder of Tiberius Gracchus in 132, the last full-scale civil war had ended with the victory of Sulla in 82. Middle-aged men whose youth had been overshadowed by the dread proscriptions were extremely reluctant to start again on the dreary round of murder and confiscation. Throughout the year 50, though sides were being chosen and forces arrayed, the three factions, Optimates, Cæsareans, and Pompeians, strove earnestly to patch up a peace. But it was ominous that these last two party-names now came into use. The Optimates stood for a principle, and a sensible one, though it is out of favor at the present day: that citizens should be undisturbed in their private lives, and free to follow the political parties of their choice, even if that entailed a weak, incompetent, and corrupt central government. But the Populars, who had once held the opposite opinion, that a majority has the right to coerce an unwilling minority, were now split into purely personal factions; their only program was to get power for a leader, who would then reward his faithful followers.

There may have been a hope that the Triumvirate could be reconstituted, with the Optimate party taking the place of the slain Crassus. But a fatal bar to any new combination was the constitutional rule which barred

Cæsar the pro-Consul from entering Rome, while Pompeius attended the Senate regularly. Pompeius was a dignified nobleman of the old school, and he was soon on good personal terms with the rest of the nobility; Cæsar, even at the age of fifty, was still thought of as a flighty young rake, an advocate of subversive ideas. In fact, his heavy responsibility in Gaul had sobered him. But few Senators had met him, save for the brief conference at Lucca, since he left Rome for the army more than eight years earlier. He was remembered as the spendthrift Ædile, not as the sound administrator of new territory. It was inevitable that Pompeius and the Optimates should drift into a close alliance against him.

The Consuls for 50 were both Optimates, or at least they had been elected as such. But one of them, Lucius Æmilius Paullus, a noble of most distinguished family, was so deeply in debt that he was open to persuasion by Cæsar's purse. A friendly Tribune was even more important, as he could veto hostile legislation; the Tribune Caius Scribonius Curio became quasi-official leader of the Cæsarean party and envoy of his master at the seat of government. Curio was a Cæsarean of the type that frightened respectable Optimates; wellborn and profligate, he had first been bought in the same way as Æmilius Paullus; but he was by this time genuinely devoted to his chief.

The summer of 50 passed in peace, while Cæsar drew up the fundamental law of his new province and Pompeius dispatched his newly trained legions to Spain. Even the elections were peaceful, and the Consuls

chosen for 49 were two more sound Optimates. The
party-leaders had until the end of the present year to
arrange some compromise. The Optimates suggested
that both Cæsar and Pompeius should lay down their
commands on the same day; but that would have left
the Optimates supreme, and Pompeius, who knew what
the Senate could do to a distinguished general after he
had dismissed his army, refused the suggestion. He proposed that Cæsar's command should be extended until
November 49. That seemed to make things safe, for
Cæsar would still be commanding his army when he
was elected Consul in July 49; but in fact it left a gap
of more than a month at the end of the year, and Cato
announced that he would then prosecute him for his old
misdeeds of 59.

The Optimates were genuinely a group of like-
minded men, without a leader or a caucus to give them
orders. So they moved slowly, and took their time in
deciding what to do next. Two possibilities pointed toward peace. In the first place, Cæsar might after all come
quietly back to Rome. Cato threatened prosecution,
certainly; but Cato was often in a minority of one. If
Cæsar peacefully stood his trial and won an acquittal,
he might continue as one of the leaders of Rome until
he died in his bed. But he would be *one* of the leaders,
and he wished to be supreme. In the second place, though
Cæsar might wish to rebel, perhaps his army would not
follow him—as the eastern army had once refused to follow Lucullus. The legions of Sulla had marched at the
word of command, but that was to put down the shame-

ful anarchy of Cinna; now Rome was freely governed by her most respected families, in alliance with her greatest soldier. No Optimate imagined that his party could be hated by decent Roman legions.

This second possibility was so inviting that the Optimates explored it, and found confirmation of their most sanguine hopes. The obvious man to consult about the feeling of Cæsar's army was his second in command, Labienus, now legate in Cisalpine Gaul. Labienus was of such obscure birth that he could have entered politics only as an extreme Popular; in fact, he shared the Optimates' reverence for the ancient families whose rule had made Rome great. He himself preferred to be governed by noblemen, and he informed the Senate that Cæsar's army would be loyal to the constitution. He was completely sincere, but he was no longer in touch with the sentiments of his men.

But the most encouraging sign, for those who hoped for peace, was that neither side prepared for war. Pompeius was at last sending off his legions to Spain, and Cæsar kept all his troops north of the Alps, save for one legion in Cisalpine Gaul which was the normal support of the Illyrian frontier. There might be trouble in the spring, but the whole winter remained for negotiation.

Therefore when the Tribunes laid down their office on the 9th of December there still seemed plenty of time for politics. On the 2nd of December the Consul Marcellus had appointed Pompeius his legate "for the defense of Italy against invasion," a precautionary move which gave him the right to draft citizens in case of emergency; the Tribune Curio tried to veto this, but his veto was ignored. On the 9th itself the Senate resolved that Cæsar must lay down his command on a date to be announced, on pain of outlawry. A newly elected Tribune, the young Cæsarean leader Marcus Antonius, interposed his veto. Not only was this veto ignored, but the sacred person of the Tribune was threatened.

The debate continued, until on the 7th of January the Tribunes Marcus Antonius and Quintus Cassius Longinus, accompanied by the ex-Tribune Curio, fled northward from Rome in real or pretended fear of death.

This injected a question of principle into what had been a naked struggle for power. It might be said that with the disappearance of any practical distinction between Patricians and Plebeians the Tribunes had lost their function; but "The Tribunes in Danger" was still a stirring Popular war cry, all the more stirring because it appealed only to ancestral memories. When the refugees reached Cæsar he determined to open the war. On the 10th of January 49 (by the calendar then in use) he crossed the Rubicon, the little stream which divided his province of Cisalpine Gaul from Italy; by so doing he proclaimed himself an aggressor and an outlaw.

It still seems a pity. Cæsar could win only by crushing the personal liberty of every other Roman, and he crushed it so successfully that since his day personal liberty has been very rare in the Mediterranean world. Both autocracy and the equally despotic system by which 51 per cent of the voters consider themselves entitled to dispose of the lives and property of the other 49 per cent

stem from the strong government Cæsar founded. Hitherto the Romans had displayed a natural genius for working a weak government, and, as the fathers of the United
States Constitution understood, liberty is safe only where
the government is weak. If Cæsar had obeyed the law,
coming home as a private citizen, probably he would
have faced nothing worse than exile (if his famous eloquence did not win an acquittal). But wild talk from
hotheaded young Optimates had convinced him that his
life was in danger, and he determined to fight for it.

His great decision was very hazardous. He had only
one legion south of the Alps, while eight others held
down conquered Gaul. Pompeius had eleven legions,
counting the two destined for Syria, and he also held
Italy, the main recruiting-ground. Most of the Pompeian
army was in Spain, but the Senate controlled what the
Romans had of a navy, and their reinforcements could
reach Italy by sea faster than infantry could march overland from Belgium. Later writers embroider stories of
Cæsar's supernatural visions before he crossed the fatal
Rubicon; but Cæsar was in fact immune to the supernatural. Once, before a battle, the ox he was about to sacrifice escaped from the altar; but even that terrible omen,
indicating that the gods rejected his offering, did not
induce him to delay his assault. In fact, as he marched
south through the winter weather the only office he held
was that of Pontifex Maximus, High Priest of Rome,
and he claimed the obedience of his troops in virtue
of it.

As the calendar was then about seven weeks fast, the

10th of January was by the sun the end of November, a time when Roman generals normally sought winter-quarters. The authorities in Rome knew they were goad-ing Cæsar to rebellion, but they counted on another three months for mobilization. Yet sixty-five days after he had crossed the Rubicon Cæsar was master of all Italy.

Before setting out he had made the usual Roman speech of encouragement to his army, which consisted only of the Thirteenth Legion. It comprised only two points: that the Optimates had disregarded the veto of the Tribunes; and that the Ultimate Decree, with all the vague menace that implied to honest Populars, had been invoked against him by the Senate. In reminding his hearers of the lynching of Saturninus and Glaucia, Cæsar seemed to range himself on the extreme left wing of the Popular party. But when he found that the veterans of the Gallic conquest cheered only for Cæsar and would follow him in any cause, he reverted to his natural posi-tion in the center.

Pompeius had once boasted, when a cautious Senator pointed out that he had few troops in Italy, that he had only to stamp his foot for armed men to spring from the ground. He found it a slower business than he had expected. The veterans who had followed him against Mithridates had been dismissed to their bonus farms more than ten years before; they still cheered for Pompeius Maximus, but many were past military age and others were reluctant to start campaigning in midwinter. The only legions he had in Italy were the two recently stolen from the army of Gaul, who could not be trusted to fight

den: "Home we bring the bald adulterer. Romans, lock your wives away." The respectable nobles gathered in Capua were strengthened in their resolve to resist to the death, rather than submit to a tyrant who thus boasted of his wickedness.

Cæsar assembled a rump of Senators, Populars and neutrals who had remained in Rome when the Optimates fled southward. He wished to regularize his position by a grant from this Senate, but Optimate Tribunes vetoed every proposal. After eleven days he marched against Pompeius; in law he was still a public enemy who had forfeited his right to command by leaving his province against the instruction of the Senate.

Pompeius was in a difficult position. He could not hold Capua against the army of Gaul and the host of new Popular recruits. He himself had an experienced staff, and most of his Optimate allies were magistrates who had held minor commands in the field; he had all the apparatus for training a good army, but unfortunately he had no recruits to train. He must retreat from Italy, either to the west, south, or east. In the west lay his own army of Spain, whose loyalty could be trusted. But Spain, wasted by recent conquest, was poor; too poor to pay an army with the punctual lavishness demanded by civil war. Africa also obeyed him, or rather it obeyed the Optimates; but Africa also was poor, and Pompeius feared to find himself once more at the mercy of the Optimates. But Greece and Asia were the theaters of his great victories. East of the Adriatic he was revered as the conqueror of Mithridates; and Asia was accustomed to raising large sums of money in a hurry, as the only way of pacifying rapacious local tyrants. Pompeius decided that he needed money more than recruits. He moved from Capua to Brindisi, prepared to cross the Adriatic. Cæsar at once blockaded the landward side of the town; without fighting a battle, merely by hard marching, he had brought the Cæsarean army to a central position, interposing between Pompeius and his faithful legions in Spain.

Pompeius might have come to a wrong strategic decision, but he was still a very great general. With weaker and half-trained forces he accomplished his embarkation while in contact with the enemy, one of the most difficult operations of war. On the 17th of March he sailed eastward, giving up his last foothold in Italy. It was only ten weeks since Cæsar had crossed the Rubicon.

Cæsar's next task was to ensure the loyalty of Rome. His amazing common sense, unfettered by prejudice or preconceived ideas, quickly restored the City to order. There were still Cæsareans who hoped, and Optimates who feared, that he would plunder the wealthy and cancel all debts; instead, he devised a new and sensible law of bankruptcy. He appointed the ex-Prætor Marcus Æmilius Lepidus Præfect of the City, with the duty of maintaining order, while Antonius commanded in all Italy. By the end of April Cæsar was free to march northward, picking up the last detachments of his Gallic army on his way to conquer Spain.

Meanwhile the dominions of Pompeius dwindled of their own accord. When the people of Sardinia heard

that Cæsar had appointed a new governor they spon-
taneously drove out their unpopular Optimate ruler; at
the same time Cato found himself unable to hold his
pro-Prætorship in Sicily against Curio, who led an expeditionary force composed of Pompeian garrisons which
had come over to Cæsar. But when Curio, still leading
the doubtful army whose nucleus was the turncoats of
Corfinium, ventured into Africa, he was defeated and
killed by the Optimates. Even so, Cæsar was strengthened. Though Pompeius had at his command the Roman
navy, which blockaded the Adriatic, Rome could not
starve while Sicily sent corn. More than anything it was
the unrelenting speed of this steady advance which un-
manned and terrified the Optimates.

The proud Greek city of Marseilles was not grateful
for Cæsar's conquest of the savage interior of Gaul, and
in the past Pompeius had been friendly to its citizens;
Domitius Ahenobarbus had gone there to take charge
of the garrison, and Cæsar found the town a hostile
strongpoint on his main line of communications. He left
it blockaded while he pressed on to the Spanish frontier.
By the 23rd of June he was on the Pyrenees with the
main army of Gaul, and within six weeks he had compelled the surrender of the whole Pompeian force. At
Ilerda, a day's march north of the Ebro, he had been cut
off from his supplies by the sudden flooding of a river
in his rear; but when all seemed lost and the Optimates
of Spain were exchanging congratulations with their
supporters in Rome, Cæsar remembered the wicker cor-
acles he had seen in Britain; setting his men to make

similar contraptions, he restored his line of supply. Then he pressed the Pompeians back and back, by sheer hard marching and the daring use of entrenchments. The pay of the opposing legions was in arrears, their families in Italy were in enemy hands, and they flinched from the onset of the veteran conquerors of Gaul. Their morale collapsed suddenly, in the manner typical of over-stretched Roman soldiers, and they compelled their leaders to surrender at discretion.

Cæsar's Spanish campaign of 49 is in one sense the highwater mark of his genius. In particular the way he compensated for inferior numbers by the use of entrenchments is characteristic of his levelheaded daring. Once again he demanded the utmost from his men, but never demanded more courage or endurance than they possessed. Yet it was a small war, without important battles, too small to be related at length in this short book.

On his return to Italy Cæsar halted to receive the surrender of Marseilles, battered to pieces after a siege in which both sides had displayed exceptional gallantry; Domitius himself escaped at the last minute, putting to sea in a storm which had driven the blockading fleet to shelter. The city was spared, as had been the Pompeian army in Spain. Cæsar was in fact merciful throughout the Civil War; but to no effect, for mercy was never expected from him.

During his absence in Spain the Roman Senate had at last regularized his position. The elections for 48 were due, but there were no magistrates to preside over them. The unprecedented dilemma was solved by an unprecedented law; instead of nominating an Interrex, the Senate appointed Cæsar Dictator to hold the Consular election. Naturally, no Optimate candidate dared to appear, and Cæsar announced that the Consuls-elect for 48 were himself and his follower Publius Servilius Vatia. He found time to enact a few sensible laws, of the kind that are obviously needed and yet very difficult to get through a popular assembly; their ancestral estates were at last restored to the heirs of Sulla's victims, and Cisalpine Gaul was declared a part of Italy. Then, having "defeated an army without a general," as he said himself, he set out eastward to conquer "a general without an army."

While Cæsar overran Spain, Pompeius had been raising money from the wealthy east; ships also he could collect, and specialized troops, cavalry, and archers. But stout Latin-speaking swordsmen came only from Italy, Gaul, or Spain; the ranks of his eleven legions were filled with poor material. His numerous and experienced subordinate officers were also more difficult to handle than Cæsar's devoted partisans. The Optimates were his allies, not his followers; the basis of their philosophy was that one noble Roman was as good as another, and the several ex-Consuls on his staff thought themselves as good as their leader, himself no more than an ex-Consul. His officers had left their homes, and in many cases their families, in Italy; they were eager to fight at once and get back again, while some Optimates suggested that Pompeius was dragging out the campaign because he wished to keep his supreme command. In fact, Pompeius, a very fine soldier, saw that his chief asset was his full war chest; he was rather a strategist than a leader of desperate charges, and he knew that in a civil war the enemy's public opinion is as valuable an objective as the enemy's commander. His plan was to drag out operations while his fleet brought hardships to blockaded Italy; Cæsar's army, which had been on active service for eleven years, must soon clamor for peace and demobilization. The general's caution and the impatience of his staff caused friction; often the compromise between two good but opposed plans of campaign was itself a piece of unsound strategy.

Cæsar's army, on the other hand, was at the peak of its morale. The men had known the pleasure of deserved glory when they saw their leader Dictator of Rome; one big battle, and the victors would dispose of the plunder of the Mediterranean world. Volunteers offered to serve without pay, and centurions contributed their stipends to hire mercenary horse. Cæsar himself displayed all his old greatness; at the age of fifty-one he could outmarch his own scouts, sleep on the bare ground, starve with his hungry legions, and dismiss dangerous grumbles with a bawdy joke. The small army he led from Rome to Brindisi was one of the most magnificent forces the world has seen, comparable to Napoleon's Old Guard or the fabulous Army of Northern Virginia.

Cæsar's old rival Bibulus held the Adriatic for Pompeius. But Roman warships were unsuitable for blockade; a vessel moved solely by oars was so crammed with rowers and marines that it could carry fresh water for only a few days, and the crew could not sleep in comfort unless they went ashore for the night. In January 48 Cæsar slipped across the Adriatic with seven legions, and though Bibulus caught some of his empty transports on the return journey, killing their captive crews as traitors to Rome, Pompeius was forced to concentrate his army for a winter campaign.

The coast towns of Epirus were held by small Pompeian garrisons, but the citizens refused to be embroiled in a Roman civil war. They compelled the soldiers to surrender, or arranged that they should march out by one gate while Cæsar entered by another. But Bibulus still kept the sea, and when Pompeius came up with the main Optimate army the little expeditionary force, cut off from Brindisi, was in a dangerous position.

From January to March Cæsar clung to his exposed foothold. Meanwhile Marcus Antonius and his brother Lucius were making desperate efforts to ferry reinforcements across the narrow sea. Bibulus is usually remembered as a touchy old fusspot, but he was also a Roman noble, with the Roman toughness and devotion to duty; like Cæsar, he was in his fifties, but he sailed the winter sea, on a wet and tossing war galley, until in March he died of exposure and privation. With the admiral dead, the blockade weakened; Marcus Antonius brought over the rest of Cæsar's army soon after Pompeius had moved up to protect his base at Durazzo.

During the winter Cæsar attempted to visit Italy to hasten his reinforcements. While Bibulus sheltered from a storm he sailed almost alone in a small but seaworthy fishing-boat; as the storm increased, the Greek fishermen began to panic, and Cæsar reminded them, in words that have endured, that "no storm could sink the boat that carried Cæsar's Luck." But even he could not complete the journey.

Once the two armies had made contact Pompeius behaved with caution; he hoped to starve the Cæsareans into retreat, while his own ships brought supplies from the wealthy east. But Cæsar noted that the enemy's numerous cavalry would need room for grazing; he decided to rely on starvation also. Pompeius was encamped by the shore, in a plain surrounded by hills; Cæsar began digging trenches on these hills, to shut him in. Pompeius threw out saps to break the line of trenches, and for weeks the two greatest soldiers in the world fenced with spades instead of swords, in a battle of wits that still commands the attention of studious generals.

Pompeius had time on his side, for Rome was growing restless. Marcus Cælius Rufus, Prætor Peregrinus (judge of commercial cases involving foreigners), led the extreme Populars in an effort to cancel all debts; after his arrest Milo, who had been exiled for the murder of Clodius, bobbed up to lead an Optimate insurrection in southern Italy; he was killed in a skirmish before his revolt could get properly under way, and the Consul Servilius ruled in Rome. But Cæsar must win the war quickly or lose it in the Forum.

With amazing self-confidence he offered battle outside Durazzo, though his forces were greatly outnumbered. Pompeius refused to fight, except for small encounters in the forward trenches. One of these brought about a striking incident; the Pompeians captured a trench, and their officers, in high delight, showed Pompeius himself the loaves of bran mixed with grass which were the only rations of the starving Cæsareans. Pompeius was not at all encouraged; he knew that his own men would desert before they would face such hardship. He gave orders that the miserable fodder of the enemy should not be shown to his troops, "for they would be disheartened if they learned they were fighting animals, not men."

But even Cæsar could not shut in much more than his own numbers of trained Roman troops led by a great general. He realized just in time that he was asking too much of his men; before they could lose heart he changed his whole plan of campaign, abandoned the blockade of Durazzo, and led his army eastward to face Metellus Scipio, who was bringing reinforcements from Asia to the camp of his son-in-law. This left Pompeius free, and some of his supporters urged him to make a dash for Italy. But that must have brought on a decisive battle, and Pompeius was beginning to lose his nerve; he played for safety by following in the steps of his adversary, and presently moved south to a strong position between Larissa and Pharsalus, covering his main base in Greece.

Cæsar had lately been so merciful that the idea got about among the little towns of Thessaly that it was quite safe to declare for Pompeius, asking quarter when the Cæsareans arrived; Cæsar put that right by sacking the defiant city of Gomphi, permitting his men to massacre the inhabitants. The results were an easing of his diffi-

culties of supply and a revival of stories about his legend-
ary ruthlessness. This is a problem Cæsar never solved.
Other things being equal, he preferred mercy; but this
side of his reputation seemed to encounter a blind spot
in his mind; he never grasped the extent of the loathing
and terror his calculated cruelty inspired.

It was now August, and the war was going as Pompeius wished. Presently Cæsar's unpaid volunteers would
lose their enthusiasm, and Rome was becoming increas-
ingly restless behind him. But the Optimates clamored
to go home, and the less they knew of war the more certain they were of victory. Now that Scipio had joined
his leader, the combined army made up 45,000 legionary foot and 7,000 good cavalry. Against this host Cæsar
had only 22,000 foot and 1,000 indifferent horse. To
civilians who counted heads it all looked very easy; only
Pompeius and the experienced soldiers in his camp knew
that every Cæsarean was worth two Pompeians. Once
again disgruntled noblemen accused Pompeius of prolonging the war merely to prolong his own command;
against his better judgment he was goaded to offer battle.

The Battle of Pharsalus was a stubborn encounter between two highly trained armies, both using the same
tactics, in which extended lines of swordsmen fenced as
individuals. In this form of fighting the skill and experience of the veteran had full play, and Cæsar had thought
out certain innovations to compensate for his inferiority
in horse. He mixed infantry with his cavalry, following
the custom of the Gauls; and he instructed his legions to
use their javelins as pikes, not as missiles, when they were

charged by the enemy horse. As a result, his favorite Tenth Legion just managed to repel the great cavalry charge with which Pompeius opened the battle. Then the whole Cæsarean line advanced against the foe. Pompeius, distrusting the skill of his recruits in maneuver, had ordered them to receive the attack halted and in silence, which naturally lowered their spirits. In addition they were so certain of victory that each unit left the fighting to its neighbors. The Cæsareans, on the other hand, knew that they were fighting a decisive battle against great odds; they were under the eye of the leader they adored; and as they advanced against more than twice their own numbers they thought chiefly of glory.

Cæsar relates a characteristic anecdote. Until his retirement Caius Crastinus had been first centurion of the Tenth Legion; he had now rejoined the army as a volunteer. Before the advance he called to Cæsar: "My lord, today you will be proud of me, whether I live or die." He charged in the front rank, pierced the enemy's line, and died from a swordthrust in the face as victory was won. An honorable remembrance was all he sought, and he has it while letters endure; but as letters now decay and courage should always be honored, I have repeated his name in this English tale.

The battle stood from dawn to midday, two long lines of men fencing with the deadly Roman broadsword. But Cæsar, always demanding the utmost from his troops, held his third line in reserve until the Pompeians were fully engaged. When this third line charged, Pompeius saw his legions break. He had gone into battle fearing defeat, and now his veteran courage deserted him. While his men still fought he fled to the camp; there he retired to his tent, overwhelmed by the first defeat he had encountered in forty years of active service.

The beaten Pompeians could not even hold the ramparts of their camp; although they had fought under a blazing sun for more than six hours the Cæsareans stormed the palisade. When all was lost the bravest Pompeians retired in a body to a neighboring mountain, and, though Cæsar cried: "Spare your fellow citizens!" as his men broke in, 15,000 Romans were killed in the pursuit; among them Lucius Domitius Ahenobarbus, perhaps the bravest and most energetic of Cæsar's enemies. Pompeius fled alone to the coast, jumped on the first ship he could find, and sailed for Lesbos, where he had left his wife. The Pompeian fugitives discovered that their mountain refuge had no water, and surrendered after a thirsty night. The whole army that fought at Pharsalus was destroyed, either dead or captive; though a few Optimates got away singly to rally in Africa, where stood the only army that had beaten Cæsareans in the field. Among these was Labienus, who was to give a great deal more trouble before he was killed.

Determined to finish the war, Cæsar at once set off by the great road to Asia. Near Salonica he learned that Pompeius was in Lesbos, and pressed on the faster to forestall him before he raised another army with Asian money. But Asia did not wait for Cæsar's arrival; in this pointless civil war the subject cities thought only of joining the winning side, and the news of Pharsalus told them which side had won. Caius Cassius Longinus surrendered the Pompeian fleet in the Dardanelles to Cæsar's advance guard, and when he learned that the great city of Antioch, capital of Syria, had declared for Cæsar, Pompeius, who had now reached Cyprus, gave up hope of raising another army and sought asylum in Egypt.

Egypt was in its normal condition of anarchy. The last king had left four children, two boys and two girls, who were fighting among themselves for the throne; in addition, Alexandria was occupied by a small Roman garrison, originally placed there by Crassus. These troops had been neutral in the Civil War; now they thought it might pay them to cultivate Cæsar; as Pompeius stepped ashore to visit the camp of King Ptolemy XII he was murdered by a Roman centurion and a Greek courtier. It was thirteen years to the day since he had celebrated his Triumph over Mithridates, and for all those thirteen years he had been the greatest man in Rome.

CHAPTER SEVEN

THE END OF THE OPTIMATES

SO LONG AS he feared that Pompeius might raise another army Cæsar advanced overland through Asia. But in September he had word that his great antagonist had sailed south from Cyprus; his destination must be Egypt. Meanwhile every great temple in Asia and Syria reported utterances by venerated statues of the gods which showed that priests and people were eager to win the gratitude of the victor by declaring for him before his troops marched in. There was no need for a formal occupation of Asia, but it was still important to capture the fleeing general before he made contact with the Optimate army in Africa. Cæsar pressed his pursuit to the uttermost.

He had with him only two legions, so weakened by hard fighting and swift marching that together they made up barely 3,200 men; with this tiny force he sailed in a scratch fleet of commandeered merchant ships directly for Alexandria. It was an amazingly bold adventure, as bold as his first invasion of Britain; and once again he thrust himself into a dangerous situation, where only his tactical skill and his genius for handling Roman troops saved him from utter disaster.

When he reached harbor he was informed of the murder of Pompeius. Northwest winds made it impossible to sail for Rome, as prudence demanded; and once his troops were landed in Alexandria he was caught up in the bloody and complicated politics of Egypt.

The Egyptian peasantry had been serfs since the first Pharaoh ascended the throne, as they are serfs today; they tilled the soil and paid their taxes. But the proud Greek city of Alexandria was notorious for the savagery of its mob, and intensely jealous of Egyptian independence, as Egypt was the only one of the Greek kingdoms founded by Alexander the Great which had not yet succumbed to Roman arms. The small Roman garrison was reluctant to receive Cæsar; these bad troops had preserved a profitable neutrality throughout the Civil War, and resented the arrival of a general who might make them work. The mob was outraged by an error of taste, which Cæsar seems to have committed inadvertently; he was extremely clever at keeping the devotion of his followers, but he often made these errors of tact in dealing with the public opinion of strangers. He marched through Alexandria with his Consular insignia borne before him, implying that his authority extended to Egypt. While the sulky garrison looked on, the mob threw stones at the emblems of foreign authority.

Of course a city mob could not harm even a small detachment of Cæsar's Gallic veterans; but in addition to the Roman garrison the little country contained three warring armies, Greek mercenaries hired to serve in the endemic civil wars of the ruling house. Of the late king's four surviving children, his elder son, Ptolemy XII, lay at Pelusium about to fight his elder sister Cleopatra, while Arsinoë, the younger sister, gathered her men to fall on the loser. (The younger Ptolemy was still in the nursery.)

During October Cæsar, in Alexandria, tried to en-force peace on the armies at Pelusium. He claimed a legal right to interfere, as the late king, Ptolemy Auletes, had asked Rome to enforce the terms of his will. But when the entire royal house was summoned to plead be-fore a foreign tribunal in their capital city, Alexandrian pride could not endure the insult. Cæsar imprisoned young Ptolemy XII in the royal palace; but the boy's soldiers, to the number of 20,000, made common cause with the discontented Roman garrison to besiege the Consul and his two weak legions. There was fierce fight-ing under the palace walls and on the great jetty adjoin-ing, where lay a squadron of surrendered Pompeian war-ships.

Historians have puzzled endlessly over the question of why Cæsar wasted time in Egypt while the Optimates rallied in Africa and reconquered Spain. There seems to be no rational explanation. But Cæsar was beloved by his soldiers, among other reasons, because he sometimes risked his life for fun. He was on the crest of the wave, soon to be undisputed ruler of Rome (where, on the news of Pharsalus, he had been declared Dictator, Con-sul, and Tribune for the next five years, with Antonius as his Master of the Horse and commander of all Italy). He felt that he could do anything; and since that storm in the Adriatic he had known, without a rational foundation for his knowledge, that his life would be spared until he had set the world to rights. The street fighting, the sud-

den diplomatic coups, the danger and the luxury of defending a splendid royal palace stocked with strong wine
and delicate food, made a swashbuckler's paradise which
brought out the last flickers of his gay and riotous youth.
Cæsar was now fifty-two years of age, and when he ruled
in Rome his fellow citizens would insist on decorous
behavior; but in his own eyes it was not so long since he
had inflamed mobs in the Forum and shocked his conventional elders by the extravagance of his dissipation. While
he led assaults on the great mole, swimming for his life
after his little dinghy swamped, while he charged through
a shower of roof tiles to clear the Egyptians from a barricaded wine shop, while he helped his men hurl javelins
and inlaid furniture from a state reception hall on the at-
tackers below (with a cold buffet, well stocked, standing in a sheltered corner), he was enjoying adventures
which are the dream of every able-bodied senior officer.
It was a frivolous waste of time, and probably he was
never happier in his life. The Valhalla of the Norsemen
is a pale reflection of Alexandria in the year 48.

The besiegers were not united. The revolted Roman
garrison were frankly brigands, but the Greek mercenaries were divided into supporters of Ptolemy, Cleopatra, and Arsinoë. At first the sisters combined against
their brother in the palace; then Cæsar sent out young
Ptolemy under safe-conduct to increase the confusion,
and Cleopatra had herself smuggled in hidden in a bale
of carpets. Cæsar at once fell passionately in love with
her.

In the New Year the Roman garrison of Syria marched

south and easily cleared up the Egyptian situation. Cæsar was now all for Cleopatra; after her partisans had killed her brother Ptolemy XII she was married to her younger brother Ptolemy XIII, in accordance with royal Egyptian custom; but the son she bore soon after was named Cæsarion. Arsinoë was exiled to Italy, and Cleopatra remained undisputed Queen of Egypt. Until June 47 Cæsar continued his honeymoon, sailing up the Nile to inspect ancient monuments like any tourist.

He was recalled to duty by trouble in Asia. Pharnaces, son of Mithridates, crossed the Black Sea from his ancestral kingdom of Bosporus (the Crimea); in Pontus he was joined by the old subjects of his father, and the resulting army defeated Cnæus Domitius Calvinus, whom Cæsar had left as legate in those parts. Cæsar encountered the victorious Asiatics at Zela, and later described the action in three celebrated words: *"Veni, Vidi, Vici"* (I came, I saw, I conquered). He first used the phrase in a private letter, and then savored his creation like any other literary man; he used it again in his official report to the Senate, to the annoyance of the more dignified Senators, and later, at his great Triumph, a placard bearing those three words was the only trophy devoted to Zela. In fact he was disappointed at the poor fight put up by the once-famous warriors of Pontus, and let fall some ungenerous remarks about the feeble foes whose defeat had brought fame to Pompeius. But Pharnaces was not Mithridates.

The defeated king was, of course, murdered by his most trusted general, in accordance with the accepted pattern of Asiatic dynastic politics. In a few days Cæsar rearranged the map of Asia, rewarding those native rulers who had been faithful. Pontus never again disquieted the Romans. Now there was nothing to detain him in the east, and Cæsar returned to Rome, perhaps reluctantly. It was a splendid thing to be ruler of the world, and unless he ruled Rome he could not rule the world; but the eastern Greeks, accustomed to the vagaries of the successors of Alexander, could make an absolute ruler happier than could his stiff-necked fellow citizens.

In September 47 he reached the City, which he had left more than two years before. It was time someone assumed the reins of power, for Rome was still as disorderly as it had been under the clumsy rule of the Triumvirs. Antonius, Master of the Horse, was nominally in command; but the disorder was led by the revolutionary fringe of the Cæsarean party, and it was no secret that Antonius, a gallant leader in the field but a spendthrift and debauchee at home, sympathized with those demagogues who wished to cancel all debts and pillage the rich. Responsibility had sobered Cæsar, but the left-wing Populars still hoped to carry out the program for which they had fought; it had been difficult to suppress Dolabella when he proposed cutting the throats of all his creditors. In addition, no elections had been held; there were no regular magistrates, and no judges to decide civil lawsuits. The Cæsarean troops in southern Italy were agitating for demobilization, with a large bonus; and they threatened to sack Rome unless it was paid immediately. In Africa the Optimates had raised a well-trained army of ten legions, while the native Spaniards had driven out their legate, Caius Cassius Longinus, the commander of the Pompeian fleet who had been pardoned on condition he served Cæsar (he had begun as a follower of Crassus, and after the death of his chosen leader he had been openly for sale).

The most pressing problem was the mutiny in Campania. But Cæsar was not only beloved by his soldiers; as an orator he was surpassed only by Cicero. When he met a deputation of mutineers in the Forum he shamed them back to their standards by beginning his speech with the word *Quirites* (voters), which placed them among mere civilians, unworthy to bear arms. It was after this speech that Cicero commented: "He speaks as well as any professional orator, who does nothing but make speeches. And look at what he does besides!"

By the end of the year Italy was under control. The long wars had of course produced a commercial crisis, when hostile armies cut off merchants from their markets. That problem was solved by scaling down all debts and canceling interest; which satisfied both the Populars, who wished to abolish debt, and the creditors, who got something when they had feared a total loss. Without election, Cæsar appointed magistrates, as was the right of a Dictator; he even set up two extra Prætors to clear off the arrears of civil lawsuits.

This was all a great deal to do in the interval of a dangerous civil war; and Cæsar offended Roman dignity by his brusque and offhand methods of settling awkward questions. His solutions were sound, but they were imposed nakedly by his sole authority. Romans did not like to see all their magistrates appointed by one man, especially when that man had come to power as leader of the party which advocated free elections; and his treatment of the Senate annoyed the respectable neutral Senators who were willing to obey a military leader if the good of the City demanded it. As most Senators supported the Optimate party, who had gathered in Africa, the Senate in Rome was very much under strength. Cæsar, as Dictator, had the right to nominate new members; but right-thinking men considered he was going too far when he appointed Gauls and Spaniards who were technically citizens, but in fact barbarians by birth; some had actually led their tribes in war against Rome, though now they were faithful Cæsareans. A wit proposed an easy way of coping with these new Senators; if no one told them the way to the Senate House these barbarous strangers would never find it by themselves. Not a bad-tempered joke, but an omen none the less; hitherto the wags had been on Cæsar's side, and Pompeius their favorite butt.

In the autumn Cæsar sailed for Africa. The season was late, and even Cæsar could not find Roman sailors who could cope with bad weather; a storm scattered his fleet, and he came ashore in the harbor of Ruspina with only half a legion. Opposed to him was the main strength of the Optimates, fourteen legions of trained Roman infantry and the numerous cavalry of their ally, King Juba of Numidia.

Now that Pompeius was dead the Optimates fought all the better. They still enjoyed the goodwill of his veterans, for what that was worth; and they were no longer hampered by an uneasy feeling that they were fighting merely to deliver Rome to one tyrant rather than another. Labienus, Cato, Metellus Scipio, Afranius, were genuinely struggling for a free republic. But as law-abiding constitutionalists they felt bound by protocol. Labienus was their best soldier, but he had never been a magistrate; therefore he could not hold a command, and the army must be entrusted to Scipio, the senior ex-Consul. The other leaders were ranked, not according to military ability, but according to their precedence in the Senate. This gave full scope to Cato, who had a genius for upsetting Roman troops and getting the worst out of them.

For three months, while he faced enormously superior numbers from his entrenched camp at Ruspina, Cæsar was in very grave danger. His men, listening to rumors of the enemy's overwhelming strength, were swept by gusts of panic. Cæsar dealt with these rumors in his own way. He made a speech to his troops. "I have heard that King Juba will soon be here with ten legions, 30,000 horse, 100,000 light infantry, and 300 elephants. Now you know as much about it as I do. So stop discussing it."

Laughing at the exaggeration, his men mastered their fears.

Several times Labienus endangered Cæsar's foragers; but he was never allowed a free hand, and as reinforcements dropped in from Italy through the usual jerky and spasmodic efforts of incompetent Roman sailors the situation at Ruspina gradually improved. The Cæsareans were upset by a prophecy that a Scipio could never be beaten in Africa, where the great Scipio had overcome Carthage. Cæsar reduced the story to absurdity, as he had dealt with the rumor of the coming of King Juba. He fished out an obscure and foolish member of the same house, Scipio Sallutio. He gave him a minor post on his staff, and then pointed out that the prophecy must be wrong; however the battle went, a Scipio would be beaten.

By April 46 Cæsar was strong enough to fight in the open. He was still much weaker in cavalry than the Optimates, and his foot, though of better quality, were slightly inferior in numbers. He desired to give battle on a narrow front, with his flanks completely secure; and with a daring typical of his genius he advanced to the position he sought, though that allowed the enemy to cut off his retreat. Marching up a narrow isthmus, he menaced the town of Thapsus and waited while Scipio brought up the main Optimate army in his rear. Then, with both flanks on the sea, in a field too narrow to afford room for cavalry, he suddenly faced about and attacked.

No infantry in the world could stand up to the legions who for thirteen years had followed Cæsar. With a loss of only 50 dead he scattered the hostile army, and when the Numidian horse fled, the Optimate foot were exposed to a merciless pursuit. Cæsar had ordered his men to grant quarter. But they were tired of the war, and they believed they were fighting men who had already received quarter in Italy or Greece (though this was in fact true only of a few leaders); they were determined to make an end. On that day 50,000 Romans were slain, the heaviest loss Rome had suffered in war for many generations.

It was the end of the war. The Optimates must die free or live under the rule of Cæsar, and each solved the problem as his conscience dictated (for they were all brave men who fought at Thapsus; the weaklings had deserted after Pharsalus). King Juba and Marcus Petreius committed suicide; Afranius was murdered; Cato tried to rally the fugitives, and killed himself when his men refused to fight on. He died, as he had lived, by the rules of Stoic discipline; and after death he was revered as a martyr to freedom. Metellus Scipio got away to some friendly ships, which were soon overtaken by the Cæsarean fleet; when his ship was boarded he fought desperately, and stabbed himself when defeat was certain; Cæsarean marines searching their prize asked the shabby old man what had become of the enemy commander in chief. "The commander in chief is doing very well," he answered, and so died.

But to my mind Labienus and the sons of Pompeius chose the better part; for no war is really won while someone on the beaten side is willing to fight on. They reached Spain, where native rebels were willing to fight Cæsar, though they were hardly fighting for the Roman constitution. But the Optimate cause seemed crushed forever, and Cæsar returned in peace to Rome.

For the first time in thirteen years, since he had gone north after his first Consulship, he might walk within the Pomœrium in the toga of peace. He was proclaimed Dictator for the next ten years, and both Senate and Comitia fell over themselves to carry out his wishes before they were expressed. But at the outset there must be a final winding-up of the long wars. Public thanksgiving was declared for forty days (in his youth ten days had been the maximum), and he was voted a Triumph.

It was the most splendid Triumph Rome had ever seen. Cæsar was hailed as conqueror of Gaul, Egypt, Pontus, and Numidia; but he suppressed any mention of Pompeius or Cato, saying that the death of fellow citizens, though it might be necessary, could never be cause for rejoicing. Plunder and trophies from most of the Mediterranean world were carried in proud pomp, and Vercingetorix and Lucterius were brought blinking from their dungeons for one last walk in the sun; while Cæsar ascended the steps of the Capitol to give thanks to Jupiter, they were strangled. That was the ancient custom of Rome, and Cæsar was as pitiless as he was willing to pardon.

His present position in Rome was greater than any man had held since the Republic was established, and it seemed only right that his statue should stand beside the images of the Seven Kings of ancient Rome. The theory of the Senatorial Republic had been that any junior magistrate, after he had governed a small district and commanded a small body of troops, was fit for the supreme responsibility of the Consulship. But Cæsar had no equal, and the structure of the Popular party,

which appealed only to the lower classes and to dissolute
nobles threatened with bankruptcy, ensured that on his
own side he should have no equal. Marcus Antonius was
his most trusted aide, Master of the Horse and second in
the state. But Antonius was a gay young scoundrel who
could lead a charge or loot a temple; he was no help as
assistant governor of Rome, and everything that needed
doing must be done by Cæsar in person.

There was much to do. For a hundred years the government had functioned clumsily, the outvoted party
constantly appealing to force. Many necessary reforms
had been postponed for fear of alienating some section
of the electorate. The most obviously needed reform was
the extension of the franchise; but that had always been
in the program of the Popular party, and Cæsar was only
doing what was expected of him when he granted citizenship to the inhabitants of Cisalpine Gaul. The boundaries he drew up for Italy have endured more or less to
the present day.

His second great reform has also endured. In a City
governed by annual magistrates an accurate calendar was
essential, but the ancient Roman calendar was a hit-or-
miss affair. Twelve lunar months, of either 29 or 30
days, made up a year of only 355 days. This was known
to be too short, and the remedy employed was that from
time to time the Pontifex Maximus should insert a thirteenth month. If this had been done every third year the
calendar would never have been more than about three
weeks out of step with the sun; but the solemn and time-
wasting ceremony of the proclamation of the intercalary

month was often postponed by a Pontifex who was a busy politician with other things to do; and a thirteenth month was a valuable prolongation of annual office, granted only as a favor to the Consuls. Cæsar had himself been Pontifex for many years, so it was largely his own neglect that had brought disorder to the calendar; but then for thirteen years he had been absent on campaign. The net result was that by 46 the calendar was a long way out, so that the Battle of Pharsalus, which really was fought on the 6th of June, was set down as occurring on the 9th of August.

City-dwellers may not think this mattered very much; our months are arbitrary divisions, corresponding to no particular astronomical events; and if you call June August no one will be the worse. But peasants regulate their plowing and sowing by the calendar, and a man who has been taught by his father to sow his autumn wheat when the "October horse" is sacrificed to Mars will run into trouble if this festival comes round ten days earlier every year. The regulation of the calendar was an important function of the Emperor of agricultural China.

As Pontifex Maximus, and Dictator as well, Cæsar could have put right the calendar for the time being with a stroke of the pen. But his restless and inquiring mind would be satisfied with nothing less than perfection, and in this field, as in many others, he cared nothing for precedent. He commissioned the greatest astronomer of the day, Sosigenes of Alexandria, to calculate the true length of the solar year. Unfortunately this cannot be fitted neatly into days of twenty-four hours, and the best approximation possible with the instruments of the time worked out at 365¼ days. So Cæsar lengthened the months to make the year 365 days, with the extra day in each fourth February which is familiar to us. He also decided that the 1st of January should be New Year's Day for all purposes, whereas previously the Romans had hovered between that date and the 21st of March. As a final touch the Senate decreed that the month of Cæsar's birth, which was known as Quinctilis, or Fifth Month counting from March, should be called the Julian Month, our modern July.

As a result of this rearrangement the year 46 continued for 445 days; but there were no impatient Consuls-elect waiting to take office, and all passed off peacefully. In future Cæsar's new calendar would be self-regulating. (It was in fact three days too long in every four hundred years, but the Pope has now put that right.)

The war was not yet quite finished, for the Optimates were rallying in Spain. There was no longer a Pompeian party, but the sons of Pompeius joined them, bringing the goodwill of the Pompeian veterans. This opposition must be crushed before it was joined by the discontented and disappointed of the entire Roman dominions; and the only man who could crush it was Cæsar himself.

It was a weakness in his position that he had no colleagues. It seemed absurd that the ruler of the civilized world must leave the City to fight an obscure band of rebels in a barbarous province; but there was no one he could send to command in his name. In Gaul he had given independent command to Labienus, but Labienus was now the best soldier in the Optimate camp. His most faithful and energetic subordinate was Antonius, and probably Antonius could have cleaned up the Spanish war; certainly he would have fought loyalty for Cæsar. But Antonius, though his loyalty could be trusted, could also be expected to bring discredit on the Cæsarean party. As deputy-ruler of Rome during the Egyptian and African campaigns he had allied himself with the left wing of the Populars, the men whose only program was to pillage the rich and then drink the proceeds. At a time when Cicero was trying to bring about an alliance between the respectable Senators and the Dictator, who was one of themselves socially if they could forget his murky past, the flashy young cavalry-leader was a liability. Cæsar dismissed him from the Mastership of the Horse in favor of Marcus Æmilius Lepidus, who had been his subordinate as Præfect of the City. Cæsar then appointed himself Consul for the year (keeping his Dictatorship), with Lepidus as fellow Consul. A nobleman who leads the party of the mob must expect to be lonely. Cæsar saw this, and looked in his own family for trustworthy lieutenants.

That gave him a very narrow choice, for the ancient Julian house was nearly extinct. Cæsar himself had fathered only one legitimate child, Julia; and she, the wife of Pompeius, had died in childbirth with her baby. Rumor attributed to him numerous bastards, but the only one he acknowledged was Cleopatra's son Cæsarion, a foreigner whom the Romans would never obey. An only son, he had no nephews of the Julian name. But the blood of his father continued in the grandchildren of his two sisters, now dead. Lucius Pinarius and Quintus Pedius were the grandsons of Julia Major, and thus represented the senior line. Pinarius was an ass, and Cæsar soon lost interest in him. Pedius was an average but not outstanding Roman of the governing class who would not disgrace himself in a minor command; in Gaul he had been a legate, and in middle life he held an undistinguished Consulship. But he was not the man to lead a party in the cutthroat game of Roman politics.

That left only young Caius Octavius, the poor relation. Julia Minor had married beneath her, for money. By her husband, Marcus Atius Balbus, she had only one daughter; and Atia again had married beneath her, one Caius Octavius Thuricus, who was not only a moneylender by trade but, what was even more disgraceful, an Italian businessman who seldom visited Rome. However, her only son, Caius Octavius, was now seventeen years old and showing some promise. Cæsar took him on his staff for what proved to be the last campaign of his life.

As had now become his custom, Cæsar surprised his enemies by voyaging in winter. Like any other Roman, he could not move troops by sea in winter without heavy loss from shipwreck, for his sailors were just as unskillful as their enemies; but that was a price he was willing to pay for the advantage of surprise. Before that long

year closed he had landed in Spain. He left a board of
Præfects to govern the City in his absence, and Rome
now enjoyed the blessing of peace and order. But while
Cæsar was absent not a single law was proposed; for the
last Romans who had minds of their own stood at bay
in Spain, and the nervous thrice-pardoned noblemen
and ignorant provincials who made up the present Senate
dared not express an opinion until they had learned
Cæsar's views.

The memory of Pompeius was popular in Spain, and
Cnæus Pompeius, his elder son, had raised an insurrection against Cæsar's legates which had now overrun
all the further province. The Optimate headquarters
were at Córdova, where Sextus Pompeius had joined his
brother and the great soldier Labienus. Between them
they had raised and trained an army of thirteen legions,
though most of the rank and file were Spanish barbarians. Against them Cæsar brought only eight legions, but his men were veterans from the genuinely Roman army which had conquered Gaul.

After a winter of complicated negotiation with the
numerous neutral cities and tribes of Spain Cæsar went
into action before the conventional campaigning season
had opened. In the middle of February he advanced on
Córdova, and by his usual tactics of swift marching and
daring outflanking maneuvers pressed back the enemy
until they must fight a pitched battle or abandon vital
territory. Of course, as they had the country on their
side and their army was not yet fully trained, the Optimates hoped for a long skirmishing war which would

offer scope for guerrilla tactics; but when Cæsar and his
Tenth Legion settled down to marching, the foe must
stand and fight or retreat beyond the limits of geography.

At Munda, after a campaign of only twenty-seven days,
Labienus drew up his thirteen scratch legions in battle
array. Cæsar immediately led his smaller force of better
troops to the attack; all day long savage Spaniard and
veteran Roman fought it out at close quarters. For hours
victory was doubtful, but at last Cæsar himself charged
on foot before his Tenth Legion, as he had led them
against the Nervii thirteen years before. Under this attack
the Spanish line at last collapsed, and the thirteen legions
mostly died where they stood. Labienus was killed in
the battle, and Cnæus Pompeius in the bitter pursuit
which followed. Sextus Pompeius got away, but there
was not a walled town in the civilized world which was
willing to shelter him. He still commanded a few ships,
and for another ten years he kept the sea as a pirate. He
had his ups and downs, and there was a time when Antonius and Octavius negotiated with him as with an
equal. But in 35 the last remaining Optimate was executed as a common nuisance by the municipal authorities
of Miletus; his cause had been killed at Munda.

CHAPTER EIGHT
CÆSAR IMPERATOR

THE NEW RULERS of Rome maintained that the Civil War had ended at Thapsus. The campaign of Munda was the suppression of a band of Spanish rebels, assisted by a few Roman renegades who shamefully bore arms against their City. Therefore when in September 45 Cæsar returned to Rome he celebrated a Spanish Triumph; in this certain Roman prisoners were led in chains, to the scandal of old-fashioned citizens who knew the protocol. Cæsar then settled down to winter in the City, and the Senate had leisure to work out a scheme of government which would give scope for his greatness.

Rome had then stood for more than seven hundred years; but never before had the Romans recognized such extreme pre-eminence in a single individual. Cæsar's will was as undisputed in the City as was a few years ago Stalin's in Moscow; the task of the Senate was to make this clear to the meanest intelligence, without humiliating too bitterly the middle-aged nobles who had been born his equals. Every soldier in the greatest army in the world was his devoted adherent (there had been soldiers who took a different view, but they were dead). He could persuade a popular audience better than any living orator. He managed the finances of the state better than any business expert. He was a considerable engineer, who could choose the right place for a bridge or a harbor, so that the many cities he founded throve after his death. He had explored unknown lands, from Britain to the Upper Nile, until he knew more of the barbarian world than any other Roman. Although he broke the constitution right and left, he was an expert in constitutional law. A notorious scoffer and atheist, he understood the intricate ceremonial of the state religion, and the complicated ritual of divination. His deceptively simple narrative of his own campaigns has been famous as literature since it was first published more than two thousand years ago (though the verse he composed as an elegant amusement was unworthy of his greatness, and his great-nephew Augustus suppressed it so thoroughly that it has failed to come down to us). He saw every situation with a clear eye and an open mind, unhampered by that conviction that what was old must be good which stultified so much Roman effort. At the age of fifty-five he could use his sword in the front rank through a long day of desperate fighting. He could seduce any pretty woman, or drink her husband under the table. There was nothing any Roman could do that he could not do better.

All the same, his position was not easy. He lived at very close quarters with a crowd of hot-tempered retired generals and provincial governors who had been born his equals, in a City where privacy was hardly known, where the Forum and the Senate took the place of the modern private club. He had won victories and been rewarded with Triumphs, but so had many others, including his despised great-nephew Quintus Pedius. In political life he was supreme, but in social life he was a respected officeholder among a crowd of respected officeholders. It was a delicate balance, and Cæsar found it difficult to hide the reality of his power under a decent mask of equality. Wherever a group of loyal Populars gathered to cheer him there would be someone to mutter stories about King Nicomedes of Bithynia, or about the goings-on when Clodius invaded the mysteries of the Good Goddess. He was a heaven-sent general, the embodiment of Roman greatness; but every Roman noble would rather die fighting than submit to being personally ordered about by this debauched aristocrat who had once been a rake about town and a scandalously spendthrift Ædile.

In the winter of 45 Cæsar's constitutional position was that of Dictator for life and Consul-elect for the next ten years: both offices unknown to the old constitution, but perfectly understandable to any Roman, and with parallels in the past. Sulla had been both Dictator and Consul, though not for life. To mark Cæsar's special greatness the Senate could only multiply honorary distinctions, and this they did with the enthusiasm of victorious party henchmen and the florid grace of Italian flatterers. He was empowered to wear every day the embroidered robe, the scepter, and the laurel wreath of gold which a Triumphator wore only on the day of his Triumph. He was granted the sanctity of a Tribune, which made it sacrilege to harm his person. His head appeared on new coins, an honor normally reserved for the illustrious dead, though not entirely unprecedented. His

statue was set up at the public expense, another honor
rare but not unprecedented for a living hero; what was
especially remarkable was that it stood in the Capitol at
the end of a row of the Seven Kings of Rome, as though
Cæsar, after more than four hundred years of the Republic, were an eighth king. The Senate conferred on
him the honorary titles of Father of his Country, and *Imperator*.

This last word, which now means Emperor, is worth
careful examination. In the past many Romans had borne
it, for its primary meaning was "commander in chief,"
especially a successful commander in chief. When a
general gained a victory his troops "hailed him as Imperator," and that was remembered by his descendants
every time his image was carried in a funeral procession.
Crassus had been "hailed as Imperator" after his first
futile raid across the Euphrates, and indeed his chief object in that expedition had been to win the distinction.
The marines questioning poor old Metellus Scipio asked
him if he had seen "the Imperator." In strict legal theory
every holder of the Imperium, the right to give military
commands, was an Imperator while his appointment
lasted. But Cæsar, whose soldiers had followed him
when he was outlawed, obviously held the power of
command for life. The Senate was only recognizing
facts when it proclaimed him Imperator for life, with the
right to use the title in civil dress, even within the sacred
Pomœrium. A Roman then might talk of Imperator
Cæsar as merely one among several successful military
commanders; but within two generations there was only

one Imperator, the ruler of Rome. The word had acquired its modern meaning.

A young Roman noble beginning his public career in the year 45 might shut his eyes to the great change. He must still seek election as Ædile and Prætor before he could hope to hold a Consulship in Rome and rule a province as pro-Consul. But he could seek office only after Cæsar had endorsed his candidature, and then he would be elected without opposition, as in a modern "People's Democracy." For the Consulship there was not even the formality of election; Cæsar nominated both Consuls, for several years in advance. The Populars had given all power to their leader; as a result the Comitia, once the source of all power, had lost its function.

Cæsar used his great power with moderation, and with a real concern for the welfare of his fellow citizens. He declined to take vengeance on opponents who surrendered to his clemency, and when an informer raked out old Cornelius Phagito, who had blackmailed him when he was hiding from Sulla's political police, he let the scoundrel go unharmed. But the Civil War had gone on too long. This was not the Cæsar who had crossed the Rubicon five years before, eager to be friends with anyone who would help him to reform the state; now his forgiveness was more condescending than vengeance, and the implied insult was bitter for a proud Roman to bear.

As a rising politician he himself had been indifferent to insult, joining in the laughter about his scandalous behavior with King Nicomedes. Before crossing the

Adriatic for the campaign of Pharsalus he had called in
a friendly way at Cicero's country house to discuss affairs
of state with an ex-Consul who was technically his equal.
Now he was in too much of a hurry to be courteous. He
had only this one winter in which to put to rights everything in Rome; next spring he must lead his army eastward to avenge on the Parthians the ignominious death
of Crassus. He became touchy about his dignity, and
though he did not punish opposition, he displayed personal resentment when anyone dared to thwart his
wishes. Pontius Aquila, who happened to be a Tribune,
happened also to be a pedantic devotee of the old forms
of the constitution; one day, as Cæsar walked through
the streets, attended as usual by a crowd of obsequious
Senators, Aquila alone refused to rise from his seat in
homage to the great man. Cæsar, noticing this, called out
sarcastically: "Don't you approve of my pre-eminence,
Aquila? Then why don't you make me restore the old
constitution?" Such a taunt to an honest old fanatic was
in bad taste, though it might be permissible in the heat
of the moment. But Cæsar, though he would not harm
the sacred person of a Tribune, kept on nagging at the
unhappy man. He would not give his decision on any
matter (a decision which, of course, was final) without
adding: "If the Tribune Pontius Aquila grants me his
permission." It is an old saying that a ruler may treat his
people as slaves and they will love him; but if he calls
them slaves they will murder him. In thus emphasizing
to the Romans that he was their supreme ruler Cæsar
made a dangerous mistake.

He never had the opportunity to sit down quietly and draw up a long-term program for the better government of Rome. During the winter of 45–44 he was preparing for the Parthian War, and he only tried to patch things up for the one summer he expected to be away. He designated no successor; he was Dictator for life, and there seemed to be plenty of time. Antonius was once more Master of the Horse, nominally second in the state; but he was unfitted to be ruler of the Roman world. Presumably Cæsar still hoped that Calpurnia would bear him a son; he was only 55, and she was not barren, but merely the victim of numerous miscarriages. (In fact miscarriage, rather than sterility, seems the best explanation of the very small families in the Roman upper class. Ladies bandaged themselves tightly to keep a boyish figure, and perhaps there was also a deadly tradition among fashionable doctors, and a habit among the rich of eating food deficient in vitamins.)

But the Romans despised as unbusinesslike a man who died intestate, and Cæsar intended to fight a dangerous campaign. He therefore deposited with the Vestal Virgins, the traditional keepers of such things, a testament which covered immediate conditions. After very generous legacies for public purposes he left three quarters of his enormous private estate to his clever great-nephew, Octavius, and the other quarter to be divided between the stupid great-nephews, Pinarius and Pedius. If Octavius accepted the dangerous inheritance (which Roman law permitted him to refuse) he was also to be adopted into the Julian house, which would make him legally the son of Cæsar. But this important decision was recorded only in the will, which of course remained secret while Cæsar lived; in public nothing was said about it, and Octavius himself was not informed. It is evident that the arrangement was made only to cover the unlikely contingency of death in battle against the Parthians. In 44 Cæsar had not chosen a successor. Perhaps he hoped that after a few years of public order the old constitution might once more be made to function.

For he gave Rome order. One of his first acts as Dictator was to dissolve the *Collegia*, private associations which were in fact gangs of political rowdies. A gang which could not hold corporate property, and which was technically illegal, lost most of its attraction for the greedy bully. But his simplest reform was to use his power as Imperator to give the City a force of military police. Hitherto the only guardians of public order had been the Lictors in attendance on the magistrates, and it had become a traditional amusement to break their rods over the heads of these comic watchmen. Now the would-be rioter might find himself crossing swords with armed veterans of the conquest of Gaul; and there were no more riots. Besides, in a one-party state there were no more contested elections to make rioting lucrative.

Rome was kept prosperous and busy, as well as peaceful. Partly from his own purse, partly from public funds which he used as though they were his own, Cæsar financed a great program of public works. The Forum Julium was a noble and non-political meeting-place, never sullied by the now obsolete elections. The Septa

Julia was a fashionable bazaar of luxurious shops. Those
poor citizens who had not lost the habit of work found
wages in great engineering projects outside the walls, the
draining of lakes and marshes and the construction of
new roads. For the hopelessly idle there was a new start
in some Roman colony beyond Italy, where every citi-
zen-founder received a free landed estate. Overseas colonies had been a plank in the old Popular program, first
suggested by the Gracchi; with Popular support Cæsar
revived great cities which had been destroyed in the first
devastating advance of Roman arms, notably Carthage
and Corinth, both desolate for more than a century.

But in everything connected with the ownership of
land he had to tread warily, for any Roman would fight
before he would give up his farm. Luckily there were
plenty of Romans and subject-allies of Rome who had
already fought and been beaten. Communities which had
guessed wrong during the Civil War were expropriated
wholesale, in particular Marseilles and the Spanish towns
which had adhered to young Pompeius; that solved the
problem of finding bonus farms for Cæsarean veterans.
When he had composed a sensible bankruptcy code to
restore liquidity to the money market, and drawn up a
series of rather pettifogging sumptuary regulations to
make the general public behave, Cæsar might turn his
attention to Parthia, confident that Rome would be quiet
while he was in the east.

One man who was not perfectly content with the present state of affairs was Antonius. He was Master of the
Horse to a lifelong Dictator, entrusted with the special

task of governing Italy and the City while his leader was on campaign. But a Dictator had no right to appoint his successor; Antonius would feel safer if Cæsar held some greater position.

Throughout the early spring of 44 attempts were made to persuade Cæsar to accept this greater position, unknown to the constitution. It was generally believed that Antonius was behind these attempts, and the question which exercised the minds of alert politicians was whether Cæsar himself approved them; historians of the next generation remained in doubt, and the problem has never been solved. My own opinion is that Cæsar was indifferent; his whole career shows him careless of honorary distinction so long as he held the reality of power. But the Romans were not so sure.

The first straw to show which way the wind was blowing was the right granted to Cæsar by the Senate to elevate new families into the ranks of the Patricians. Something had to be done, for the number of Patrician houses was dwindling. The children of a mixed marriage ranked as Plebeians, and as many elective posts (for example, the Tribunate and one Consulship) were closed to Patricians there was a continual temptation for the politically minded to seek adoption into a Plebeian house, like the notorious Clodius. But the due worship of the gods, according to the forms of the state religion, demanded young Patricians to hold certain ancient priesthoods. It was one of those awkward political problems which had seemed insoluble until Cæsar assumed responsibility for solving it. All the same, every student of the constitution would remember that in all the seven hundred years of Roman history only kings of Rome had the power to make a Patrician.

Then, on a day when it was the custom to decorate the statues of the old kings with garlands, Cæsar's statue, standing beside them, was found decorated in the same manner. Certain Tribunes at once ordered the removal of the garlands, and their orders were obeyed; Cæsar said nothing, and even his closest supporters never knew whether he was disappointed.

The ancients had no sympathy with bodily disfigurement; if a man had only one eye, though he had lost the other fighting honorably for his city, he became automatically a figure of fun. Cæsar in his fifty-sixth year was still handsome, athletic, and graceful; but the top of his head was quite bald, and he was acutely ashamed of it. He was glad to make use of the Senate's permission to wear Triumphal ornaments every day, and was never without his laurel wreath, which hid the bald patch. Critics said it looked very like a crown.

In February Antonius was chosen as one of the actors in the queer archaic ritual of the Lupercalia. The she-wolf who had suckled Romulus was one of the sacred animals of Rome, and on this day bands of young men, the Luperci, impersonated wolves. Clad in the bloody skins of newly slain goats and brandishing whisks of bloody goat-hair, these sacred figures ran through the streets; and any woman sprinkled with the blood was considered certain to conceive brave warriors. (It is well to remember, when we picture the grave Roman standing in a noble attitude beside the altar, as shown in many marble reliefs, that his religion had this other, orgiastic, side.) Of course these Luperci, distributing blood and good luck, were permitted to roam where they would. Antonius ran up to Cæsar during a crowded show in the Circus and offered him a royal crown.

Now that the citizens assembled in Comitia could only vote for candidates chosen by the Dictator, the crowd in the Circus had taken over the duty of expressing public opinion. The people saw at once that Cæsar was testing their sentiments, and they reacted; there were roars of disapproval until it was seen that he refused the proffered crown, and then he was cheered wholeheartedly. That was, as things fell out, the last attempt to make Cæsar King of Rome; but if he had lived, Antonius would have renewed his persuasion.

The Roman horror of kingship is more easily understood by Americans than by Englishmen. Cæsar had fought his way to supreme power, which he must now hold for as long as he lived; but he had risen as the leader of a numerous party, and if the great majority of Romans had turned against him, as they might have done had he proclaimed himself king, he must have fallen.

Cæsar, though he would rule Rome for as long as he lived, could not make himself king (and in my opinion he did not want to). In fact, now that a few obvious but politically difficult reforms had been carried out, he seems to have been uncertain of his future program. Some Populars wanted a complete social revolution, or at least a division of all available wealth among poor Roman citizens only, without consideration for slaves or foreigners; but Cæsar, though he had found their votes useful, had never been one of them. On the other hand, there is one thing no Dictator can do, whatever his power: Cæsar could no more retire into private life than Stalin could go back to his ancestral farm in Georgia. For the moment there was a war to be waged against the Parthians, but when that was over the outlook was uncertain.

Certain processes, completed under the Emperors, can be traced to faint beginnings under the Dictatorship of Cæsar; notably the wide extension of Roman citizenship, and an emphasis on the welfare of the provinces which entailed some neglect of Rome as a city. But these may not have been the result of conscious policy. Citizenship was the obvious reward to offer to doubtful provincials during civil war; and after Cæsar crossed the Rubicon the capital of the Roman dominions must be the headquarters of his army, whether in Africa or Spain. Now that Cæsar had abolished the oligarchic government of the Optimates, without carrying into effect the full program of the Populars, there was nothing left but to mark time under his personal rule.

The mob adored Cæsar, and the commercial middle class was satisfied with his orderly administration. The opposition could not hope for mass support from any quarter, but inevitably an opposition was collecting. Every Roman noble thought that his birth entitled him to a short term of supreme command, yet Cæsar monopolized power. A party which has won a civil war inevitably contains ambitious men for whom the fighting ended just too soon, before they could attain the positions their capacity deserved; and others who fought only for plunder and whose greed can never be satisfied. A coalition formed, of nobles deprived of any field for their ambition, of disappointed generals holding second-rate commands, and of plain scoundrels who disliked order.

In the leadership of the conspiracy the old Optimate party was represented by Caius Cassius Longinus. He had begun his political life as a follower of Crassus; after his leader was killed by the Parthians he ranked as a not very ardent supporter of Pompeius; in the campaign of Pharsalus he had ensured his own good treatment by surrendering the Pompeian fleet to Cæsar's cavalry; Cæsar had made him his legate in Spain, that he might be committed to the Populars without hope of another change of sides. In 44 he was legate-designate in Syria, waiting to go east with Cæsar for the new Parthian campaign. He was a brave soldier, a competent though corrupt administrator, and an artful politician. He had served each Triumvir in turn, and deserted each sinking ship before his feet were wet. Cæsar did not trust him, but he could see no other leader who might lure him away; and as on other occasions he underestimated the resentment felt by noble Romans when he continually gave them orders.

Cassius had a simple grievance. He thought he should be Prætor, and the post of legate in Syria was not enough to buy his loyalty.

Marcus Junius Brutus, the other Optimate leader, was a very different type of man. *Brutus* literally means *stupid*, and though the literal meaning of these old family names had been forgotten, it suited him very well. He was the son of Cæsar's old mistress Servilia, and there were scandalmongers who said he was Cæsar's son; I have already given my reasons for disbelieving this. He had fought for the Optimates at Pharsalus, and then surrendered. He had at once been pardoned, and Cæsar trusted him. But he never forgot that his remote ancestor Lucius Junius Brutus had expelled King Tarquinius and had been elected Consul in the first year of the Republic. He read Greek history and the political theory that went with it, and he believed, as these Greek writers taught, that the best way to deal with a tyrant is to murder him. Brutus was perfectly honest and disinterested. He wished to restore liberty, and he sought nothing for himself. The other conspirators were glad to use his courage, but they did not follow his advice.

These other conspirators were all Cæsareans, either unscrupulous ruffians who hoped to enrich themselves by disorder, or military commanders disappointed of promotion. Decimus Junius Brutus had been Cæsar's legate throughout the conquest of Gaul, and seems to have been as much of a specialist in nautical affairs as the land-bound Roman army could produce. He built the fleet which defeated the Veneti in 56, and commanded the naval blockade of Marseilles in 49. He wanted some greater reward than Cæsar had so far offered him.

Caius Trebonius had never risen higher than the Tribunate, but he had been a useful Cæsarean agent in the

Comitia. In 49 he co-operated with Decimus Brutus in the siege of Marseilles, commanding the land forces; the two became close friends, and it seems that in this conspiracy he was merely following Brutus.

These men planned to murder Cæsar with their own hands in the Senate House, and they went about, with very few precautions, to bring other Senators into the plot. Publius Servilius Casca, a Tribune for the year 44, and Lucius Tillius Cimber, pro-Prætor-designate in Bithynia, were supposedly faithful Cæsareans who joined in the plot as soon as they heard of it. It was said afterward that more than sixty Senators were aware of what was planned, though some of them scrupled to play a part in it.

Why was it so easy to arrange Cæsar's murder in a Senate which he had deliberately packed with his own supporters? The rank and file of the conspirators had three guiding motives. A very few were honest Optimates who wished to restore the old rule of the Senate, recruited by free election in the Comitia. A rather larger number were ambitious Populars who expected the Populars to remain in power, but who thought they might gain promotion when everyone moved up one after the leader of the party had been removed. But the greater part were ordinary honest Romans, of noble birth and sufficient capacity to hold high office, who were thoroughly tired of being ordered about by a fellow noble. In his heart every Senator regarded the Senate as a club of equal colleagues. Any man who ruled alone could keep their loyalty only by the exercise of constant

tact, and Cæsar was now too tired and too busy to be
constantly tactful.

He was merciful, and his rule was not oppressive; but
he made no efforts to spare the feelings of his nominal
equals. As his instructions would always be obeyed in
the Comitia, no one minded his nominating magistrates
without the formality of election; but he was altogether
too casual in his nominations. For the year 47 he had
not bothered to nominate any Consuls or other magistrates; when he gave the matter his attention he would
nominate them for several years in advance, to save
trouble. When a Consul died on the last day of the year
he appointed a substitute, as though the great office were
a merely formal dignity. He broke one of the most
stringent laws of the constitution by appointing as Prætor a man who held the Tribunate, which implied that
all the magistracies of the old Republic were now equally
meaningless. Throughout his life Cæsar had blundered
in his dealings with Roman public opinion, and now
this lack of sympathetic insight was fatal.

With more than sixty politicians swearing their friends
to secrecy and opening confidential negotiations the plot
quickly became a subject of common gossip. Obscure
charlatans who pretended to foresee the future seized the
opportunity to prophesy woe; and Cæsar's most faithful
friends, his wife Calpurnia and Antonius, begged him to
take precautions. But Cæsar, all his life, had very sound
ideas on the discomforts of safety. He had seen Asiatic
kings, and he knew what a burden an ever present bodyguard can be; he also knew that a bodyguard is no real

protection, for a determined enemy may bribe some
guardsman to commit the very crime he is hired to prevent; among early Roman Emperors Caligula, Tiberius,
and Domitianus were each murdered with the connivance of the body guard. Cæsar determined to carry on
as though he were not threatened, and spoke frequently
of the horrors of a sickbed and the mercy of a quick
death. Suetonius, a much later historian who specialized
in second-hand gossip, reports a rumor that "Cæsar left in
the minds of his friends a suspicion that he did not wish
to live longer." Probably that only means that he brushed
aside fussy precautions; he still had much to do, and in
the summer there would be the great war against the
Parthians. He refused to alter his whole manner of life
to guard against what might be an imaginary danger.

On the 15th of March 44 there were several reasons
why Cæsar should not go to the Senate. He was not
feeling well, there had been a spate of unfavorable
omens, and Calpurnia had a scheme that he should stay
in his house until he could ride east to join his faithful
troops. But there was also an important ceremonial
which he ought to perform. It was the day appointed for
him to lay down his Consulship and receive the formal
pro-Consular command which authorized him to lead
the Roman army into Parthia. When Decimus Junius
Brutus called to escort him he set out for the Senate;
which still met in the Theater of Pompeius, as no one
had yet got around to rebuilding the old Senate House,
burned down in the rioting after the murder of Clodius
in 52.

He was of course completely unarmed, draped in the cumbrous toga which Roman citizens wore on ceremonial occasions. The conspirators also wore togas, but they carried concealed daggers.

As Cæsar entered, Cimber came up to present a petition. Other Senators crowded round, as though to back his request. Suddenly Casca, directly behind him, drew his dagger for the first stroke.

It was only a year since Cæsar had charged on foot with the Tenth Legion to win the battle of Munda; he was not yet fifty-six, and quite capable of defending himself. He wrapped his toga round his left arm to serve as a shield, and struck back with his *stylus*, the long iron pencil the ancients used for scribbling on wax tablets. Most of the Senators were surprised at the sudden fray, and if he had fought on for a few minutes they might have rescued him. But the story goes that he was so shocked to recognize among his assailants Marcus Junius Brutus, the son of his old love, that he ceased to struggle, hiding his face in his toga that he might not flinch from the weapons of his enemies. His last words were "You too, Brutus?" as though in realization of the emptiness of human affection.

When he fell his body bore twenty-three serious wounds. He lay at the foot of the statue of Pompeius, the builder of the Theater; it had been removed after Pharsalus, and recently restored at Cæsar's express command. The conspirators ran out to the Forum, cheering for liberty; and the rest of the frightened Senators dispersed quietly to their homes.

At first Rome received the news of Cæsar's death with indifference or relief. But at the funeral Antonius assumed command of the Populars, and, soon after, young Octavius came to the City to claim his adoption and inheritance. Thus began the long and complicated civil wars which ended fifteen years later, in 29, with the accession of Octavius, now Imperator Caius Julius Cæsar Augustus, to what had become the throne of the Roman Empire.

That story has hardly ended yet. The last Holy Roman Emperor changed his title to Emperor of Austria to please Napoleon. But meanwhile the word *Cæsar*, once the name of a private Roman family, had come in many languages to mean Emperor. The Tsar of Bulgaria abdicated in 1946, and since 1947 India has left the protection of the Kaisar-i-Hind. Yet it would be rash to say that there are absolutely no Cæsars reigning anywhere in the world.

Caius Julius Cæsar was the greatest man Rome ever produced, especially great in the versatility of his genius. He brought France into the community of nations and fixed the civilization of the Mediterranean world into the mold which still contains it. His work endures to this day.

But he had one weakness, a contempt for the self-respect of his fellow men. Intellectual pride brought him to a squalid and untimely death. It is still the most dangerous temptation of successful politicians.

NOTES FOR FURTHER READING

FOR the life and times of Caius Julius Cæsar we are well served with genuine contemporary documents. In addition the generation of Romans who came after were fascinated by his fame, and collected all the first-hand traditions old men were willing to recount. We know very much more about Rome in the first century B.C. than we do about the Empire in the third century A.D. or about Europe in general during the sixth and seventh centuries.

The primary source for Cæsar's campaigns in Gaul and Britain are his own *Commentaries*. In form these are simple jottings, notes composed each winter to inform the Senate of his doings during the previous summer. Internal evidence suggests that they were actually written year by year, and never revised before final publication. For example, at the outset the Druids are described at some length; and the description remains, though the absence of reference to them in later years shows that in fact they carried little weight in Gallic politics. In the same way the account of Britain is that which Cæsar must have received from Gallic merchants before his first expedition. By the time he left the island he would know that it was more civilized than he had been led to believe; but he allowed the early account to stand.

The style of these jottings is deceptively simple. The effect is of a bluff straightforward soldier putting down the events of the season in the order in which they occurred. In fact it is very difficult to write Latin as simple as that, and only Cæsar could do it. *Commentaries* of

the same type dealing with the Civil War and the
War of Alexandria passed in antiquity as Cæsar's work,
though they may have been written by members of his
staff. Eyewitnesses of his later campaigns in Asia, Africa,
and Spain completed the series in the best imitation they
could manage of his unique style.

Cæsar's *Commentaries* have been many times translated into English and other European languages. My
own favorite is John Warrington's version in the *Every-
man* series, a free rendering but a good story in English.
The Loeb translation perhaps gives the force of the Latin
more exactly.

Cicero wrote *Letters*, ostensibly to his friends but certainly polished for publication to the world at large.
These cover public affairs from his Consulship to the
victory of the young Octavian. They have always been
famous as perfect specimens of Latin prose, and have
been many times translated.

Tacitus and Suetonius were the chief collectors of
traditions, a century after Cæsar was dead but while his
party, the Populars, was still a going concern and interested in its great leader. Both lived in the political society
of Rome, and knew personally the political leaders of
their own day.

Plutarch, who lived in Greece, collected all the written evidence he could find, especially about Cæsar the
man; he was a trained historian who could use his documents. There are numerous translations of all these famous writers, and after reading them we ought to see a
true picture of Cæsar.

In fact we will not, for each document was written
not to make plain the truth but to expound a point of
view. Cæsar's own *Commentaries* are party pamphlets,
glossing over his unprovoked aggression against barbarians and extremely unfair to the Optimate faction in

the Senate. Cicero is prejudiced against Cæsar, and sometimes misinformed about events far from Rome; throughout he exaggerates his own importance. Tacitus wrote to
prove that the rule of one man in Rome must be slavery
for all other Romans, and that absolute power must corrupt the ruler. Suetonius, a civil servant with access to
priceless documents now perished, believed everything
he saw written down. His fondness for a smutty story has
ensured the immortality of his work, but he never noticed that the same man could not be a coward and a
miser on one page and a warrior and spendthrift on the
next. Plutarch was trying to show that Romans were
exactly like Greeks; they were not.

Nevertheless, these writers tell us what happened, for
they could not go wrong in reporting notorious public
events. We must disregard their theories and explain the
events for ourselves. We study the classics to learn how
to think.

Of modern writers about Cæsar, by far the greatest
was Theodor Mommsen. His *History of Rome* (New
York: E. P. Dutton; 1911) is accurate in its facts; but
he wrote, under the Hohenzollern Emperors of Germany, to prove that emperors are a good thing, and he is
grossly unfair to Pompeius.

The best explanation, for beginners, of the very complicated Roman constitution is still to be found in the
simple little schoolbook of Professor J. L. Myres, *A History of Rome* (London: Rivingtons; 1905).

For manners and customs Jérôme Carcopino's *Daily
Life in Ancient Rome* (New Haven: Yale University
Press; 1940) will correct the exaggerations of the
cinema.

INDEX

This book was set on the Linotype in a face called *Eldorado,* so named by its designer, WILLIAM ADDISON DWIGGINS, as an echo of Spanish adventures in the Western World. The series of experiments that culminated in this type-face began in 1942; the designer was trying a page more "brunette" than the usual book type. "One wanted a face that should be sturdy, and yet not too mechanical. . . . Another desideratum was that the face should be narrowish, compact, and close fitted, for reasons of economy of materials." The specimen that started Dwiggins on his way was a type design used by the Spanish printer A. de Sancha at Madrid about 1774. Eldorado, however, is in no direct way a copy of that letter, though it does reflect the Madrid specimen in the anatomy of its arches, curves, and junctions. Of special interest in the lower-case letters are the stresses of color in the blunt, sturdy serifs, subtly counterbalanced by the emphatic weight of some of the terminal curves and finials. The roman capitals are relatively open, and winged with liberal serifs and an occasional festive touch.

This book was composed, printed, and bound by The Plimpton Press, Norwood, Massachusetts. Paper manufactured by S. D. Warren Company, Boston. The typography and binding were designed by the creator of its type-face—W. A. Dwiggins.